Becoming an

Unstoppable

WOMAN

Mompreneur

25 RELENTLESS

SUCCESSFUL MOM ENTREPRENEURS

Table of Contents

Introduction

She Rises Studios was created and inspired by mother-daughter duo Hanna Olivas and Adriana Luna Carlos. In the middle of 2020 when the world was at one of its most vulnerable times, we saw the need to embrace women globally by offering inspirational quotes, blogs, and articles. Then, in March of 2021, we launched our very own Women's Empowerment Podcast: She Rises Studios Podcast.

It is now one of the most sought out Women's based podcasts both nationally and internationally. You can find us on any of your favorite podcast platforms, such as Spotify, Google Podcasts, Apple Podcasts, IHeartRadio, and much more! We didn't stop there. The need to establish a safe space for women has become an even deeper need. Women lost their businesses, employment, homes, finances, spouses, and more to a global pandemic.

That's when we decided to form the She Rises Studios Community Facebook Group. An environment strictly for women about women. Our focus in this group is to educate and celebrate women globally. To meet them exactly where they are on their journey.

It's a group of Ordinary Women Doing EXTRAordinary Things..

As we continued to grow our network, we saw a need to help shape the minds and influences of women struggling with insecurities, doubts, fears, etc. From this, we created a global movement known as:

Becoming An Unstoppable Woman #BAUW

The movement is to universally impact women of all ages in whatever stage of life they are in, to overcome insecurities, adversities, and develop an unstoppable mindset. She Rises Studios educates, celebrates, and empowers women globally.

In this book, you will be inspired by a collaboration between She Rises Studios and 25 powerhouse-industry leading women from across the globe who will inspire purpose-driven women to STAND OUT, RISE, and THRIVE!

The book's mantra is "Collaboration OVER Competition."

Becoming An Unstoppable Woman Mompreneur is written for Mama's who are already in business as well as for Mama's who are ready to launch themselves into the entrepreneurial world. We believe that mompreneurs are leaders in business due to their resilience, compassion, and unwavering commitment to succeed. The amazing mama authors in this book have shared their truths, hearts, secret trade secrets, and so much more on none other than Mother's Day. The #BAUW authors celebrate all around the world in the hopes of sharing inspiration and celebrating our achievements as moms.

She Rises Studios offers:

- She Rises Studios Publishing

- She Rises Studios Public Relations

- She Rises Studios Podcast

- She Rises Studios Magazine

- Becoming An Unstoppable Woman TV Show

- She Rises Studios Community

- She Rises Studios Academy

We won't stop encouraging women to be Unstoppable. This is just the beginning of our global movement.

She Rises, She Leads, She Lives...

With Love,
HANNA OLIVAS
ADRIANA LUNA CARLOS
SHE RISES STUDIOS
www.sherisesstudios.com

Hanna Olivas

Founder & CEO of She Rises Studios Podcast & TV Host | Best Selling Author | Influential Speaker | Blood Cancer Advocate | #BAUW Movement Creator |

https://www.linkedin.com/company/she-rises-studios
https://instagram.com/sherisesstudios
https://www.facebook.com/sherisesstudios
www.SheRisesStudios.com

Author, Speaker, and Founder. Hanna was born and raised in Las Vegas, Nevada, and has paved her way to becoming one of the most influential women of 2022. Hanna is the co-founder of She Rises Studios and the founder of the Brave & Beautiful Blood Cancer Foundation. Her journey started in 2017 when she was first diagnosed with Multiple Myeloma, an incurable blood cancer. Now more than ever, her focus is to empower other women to become leaders because The Future is Female. She is currently traveling and speaking publicly to women to educate them on entrepreneurship, leadership, and owning the female power within.

Go Mama Go

by Hanna Olivas

Go Mama Go! Yes, You Can Have It All

I keep telling myself "go mama go, yes you can have it all." Every day I wake up and repeat this over and over in the morning. My day usually begins at 5am. Yep, this mama is a 5am club mama. I love to use the first few quiet hours of the day for prayer, meditation, journaling, exercise, or just playing some music to get me pumped for the day. Being a mom and an entrepreneur takes balance, coffee, prayer, and skill. Mostly coffee and prayer. As soon as the 8am alarm sounds off, it's go time. My little 9-year-old Sophia is up and at 'em. I have learned that keeping her and myself on a morning schedule and routine keeps us both from going crazy. Haha, but it's true. It seems like together we are a morning comedy show. I get her to school and I have precisely calculated how many hours of work I can get done before she is out of school. I call this time blocking or time management. My time blocking starts as soon as I open my eyes. Here is a little peek into the first two hours of my day.

1) Prayer

2) Meditation

3) Journal

4) Exercise

5) Shower, get ready for the day, and a cup of my favorite Go Mama Go coffee.

Next is Go Mama Go to work for six amazing hours doing what I absolutely love and cherish. I am the CEO and Co-Founder of a global public relations, marketing, advertising, and publishing agency for women. She Rise Studios was created by women for women, to meet them on a global level. The bonus is working side-by-side with my oldest daughter, who is also the co-founder of our company. Yes, that's right, this mama can have it all. Now here is where the word "unstoppable" comes into play. No matter what life throws at me, I remain hyper focused on my unstoppable mindset and clarity to get me through the day. Because sh#t happens and we, as mothers, need to be prepared and able to juggle balls, bananas, apples, lemons, all while standing on one foot. Can you picture this? I hope so, because it happens daily. Did I mention yet that I am also the proud wife of an amazing man I've known for thirty-five years? So yes, being a mother of five children ages 9 to 30, a wife, and a hot grandma to my amazing grandsons, I am an Unstoppable Mompreneur.

So now you have the basics of what my week looks like Monday through Friday.

Let's add in the rest: homework, cooking, dinner, dishes, laundry, and my all-time favorite, grocery shopping. Ha Not!!!! I absolutely despise the grocery shopping part. I try very hard to be done with work by 4pm.

I personally require eight full hours of sleep, so I am very disciplined in getting all my Go Mama Go duties, wife, and household duties done by 7pm, then it's my time to decompress and go to sleep. If I don't sleep a full eight hours, I am now Growl Mama Growl. Sleep plays an important part in all of this. Our brains and bodies need rest and relaxation to get up and repeat five days a week. Being an Unstoppable Woman Mompreneur requires me to preplan and time block regularly. I use Sunday evenings to map out the week ahead. Have you wondered when I spend time with my family and have fun? The answer is, every day!! They are all a part of my every waking moment, whether it's a quick text, video call or a love letter in a lunch box, we make it happen. I wouldn't be successful without them.

Teamwork makes the dream work. My weekends are left wide open, and we pretty much travel when we want. The beauty of being a mompreneur is that you can create your own schedule so you can live the life you want.

Now let's talk about when sh#t hits the fan and days don't go as planned. I can't even count how many WTF moments I have on a daily basis.

What should I do? How do I react to the school calling to pick up my sick daughter, or not being able to meet a deadline for a client, or if I get sick? How about my all-time favorite? When I am in a hurry and I hit every red light possible! Ugggghhhhh!!

The answer is that life happens to us all, and we, as mothers, tend to want to fix everything and carry the burden of the world on our shoulders. However, obviously, that's impossible!! So what I say is, "it's ok..." We are human, not robots. We don't have control over everything, but we do have control over how we react to it. My gift when sh#t hits the fan is laughter. I simply chuckle and tell myself, "It's OK, Mama," because you can still have it all. Keep going; don't quit. Be still and let life's storm pass. Give yourself the grace to pick up the pieces and Go Mama Go! This is my mantra in life and business. Always find humor and laughter; it heals any situation. I want you to know that no mompreneur is perfect. We all juggle, we all make mistakes, and we all lose our balance at times. That's just life. We all look up at the sky and say "really?" like "why now?" That's ok mama, keep going, laughing and chucking it in the chuck it bucket.

I say, create the life you want to live in both life and business and make the best of it. Be the ring leader in your own circus, and never give up. You can pause, but never quit. The world needs more mompreneurs. By creating our businesses, we create income resources for millions of people annually. We inspire others by being an inspiration. We empower others by being empowered. Mompreneurs are a vital part of our economy. We are also educating society on what it takes to be a mother and run a business, be corporate, or be a working mama. All are just as important as the others. We are showing our wonder woman powers daily, breaking society's opinion that mothers should be at home with their children. Most of all, we are showing our children what it takes. They watch and learn from us.

So, yes, Go Mama Go. Yes You Can Have It All!! You do it by making a plan, blocking out time, planning ahead of time, involving your children, asking for help, seeking a coach or mentor, assembling your dream team in life and business, and, most importantly, believing in yourself, Mama!! Dream Big, Do Bigger. Live your Go Mama Go Life Without Limits. Embrace it all. Make realistic goals and plans; don't over commit. Remember, it's progress over perfection, not the other way around. Never compare yourself to another mama. Instead, look to her for inspiration, tools, and strategies; never compare. We are in this together! If you see another mama's tiara tilting, help her fix it with love.

One last thing: I call bullsh#t on those social media mamas who portray social media perfection. It's not real, so don't compete with fantasy. Keep it real, raw, relatable, authentic, and you will be just fine!!

Go Mama Go, I have faith in you! Yes, you can have it all!

All My Love,
The Go Mama Go
Hanna

Pam Kurt

Best Version of You LLC
Professional Women Networking and Life Coach

https://www.linkedin.com/in/pamela-kurt-41a26ba/
https://www.instagram.com/Best_Version_You
https://www.facebook.com/Best-Version-You-103772311530954
www.BestVersionYou.com
www.PamKurt.com

Pam is an attorney, business owner, community leader, author, speaking and MOM! Her most important job has been to raise her son Joshua. She has a new business, Best Version of You LLC to empower other women to level up and be the best they can be for themselves and their families.

Locked Out of Christmas

by Pam Kurt

Well, I am one of millions of moms that went on that journey as a single mom. I got divorced when my beautiful boy was 3 years old, and I had to start all over. I literally left Miami, Florida to go back to Ohio with my baby, a crib, and a few clothes. I didn't know that that was just the start of our journey.

I was super excited to be able to write about my single mom life. What a fitting platform. I have always figured out how to juggle this life, hence Mompreneur! Interestingly, when I look back, I am not sure how I juggled it all, from homeroom mom, to practice, to working, to law school, but I DID IT! As a single mom, you truly do what you need to do to get through.

The work life balance changes as time evolves. Throughout my life, I have been a hard worker and a multitasker. Those skills clearly became fine-tuned as the single mom thing developed. I say "robbing Peter to pay Paul" was one of my best feats. I, like most mothers, made my son my priority and life. As I look back and when we share "war stories," I am still not sure how God gave me enough hours in the day back then. I worked, went to school, was a homeroom mom, did sports, housework, and always had a side job going, everything from selling Tupperware to delivering pizzas. Yet my son would want for nothing.

We (me and my son) went through many moves and struggles. However, there are some that are truly some of our most infamous stories. When I discussed with my son which one to use for this chapter, he said, "The Christmas one!". OK, my son is now a lot older and when this was going on, he didn't even know, BUT I was sure to share when he was older. At the time, if he knew, I would have been devastated.

So, as a good mom, I separated some Christmas presents for him from Santa. I put them in an attached shed in my backyard. There was a key lock on the shed because our push lawn mower was also in there. At that time, my son wasn't the happiest guy to sleep alone. I even had to buy a motion detector power ranger to guard the bedroom door. For me, getting up in the middle of the night and walking downstairs was going to be a task. Tip toeing my way... I walked past his room, down the stairs, through the kitchen, grabbing my coat and putting on my boots to go outside. Now, picture this: I am in my pajamas, in open boots, with my coat and bedhead, walking through ice and snow to get to the shed. This quest didn't sound unreasonable but let me assure you that this walk was the longest step ever! Under the fallen snow was ice, so I was inching my way. When I got to the shed and tried to put the key in, there was ice! Not just a little bit... The entire lock and door handle were covered with this clear shine from the street light.

I went step by step back into the house. What can I do? Of course, as any resourceful mother would, you find a way! I grabbed a small pot, filled it with water (the entire time looking up in hopes he couldn't hear the water run) and put it on the stove to get warm. I was even afraid to breathe too loudly to wake him up. It felt like it took forever.

Once I saw the water was just starting to boil (I could see little bubbles), I grabbed a pot holder and slowly carried the pot to the back of the shed. I poured water on the lock. The ice melted and REFROOZE in front of my eyes. I was defeated. I walked back in and refilled the pot, put it on the stove and waited. I was sitting on the stairs, and I remember the defeated feeling. I had to try again. I have to save for Christmas.

After three times, the ice melted and I could use my key. I started to bring the gifts in and one fell in the snow. I just kept doing what I needed to do for Christmas. Damn it! I can do this and he WILL HAVE A CHRISTMAS! Once all the gifts were in place and the doors locked, I crawled back to bed, exhausted and acted like all was well in the morning.

That morning, Christmas was grand. He was surprised, and my heart was filled. Inside, I knew it was all worth it! I wasn't able to share with him one of my glorious single mom moments until years later. However, that morning, he did ask why one of his presents was wet, and I denied the whole thing and simply stated I didn't know.

There were so many incidents, but Christmas was one of the most memorable. I just know that my role as a mother is the most important and loved role in my life. No matter what I achieve in my career, I value my son and family the most. I am so glad for all of those memories and won't trade them. I wanted to share this because when this happened, I sat on the stairs waiting for the water to boil, then carrying the pot of water to the shed, and then, after dropping presents, still getting them under the tree, I felt sorry for myself. There were many tears and breakdowns. I blamed my ex, God, and myself.

But I MADE IT! You can too! Never give up and take care of your family. If you stay on the path, you can and will get there. I know that sometimes the despair is deep. Know that God will lift you up and get you through. Dream big and don't quit! To the single mothers out there, you can do this! God doesn't make anything stronger than a MOM! and I will be here rooting for you to get through, too!

Charlotte Howard Collins

Award Winning Business Growth Expert | Speaker | Best Selling
Author Publisher | Entrepreneur

www.LinkedIn.com/in/charlottehoward
www.Instagram.com/coachwithcharlotte
www.Facebook.com/coachwithcharlotte
www.charlottehowardcollins.com
www.heartcenteredwomenpublishing.com

Charlotte Howard Collins is a loving wife and mom to four beautiful children. She's an Award Winning Business Growth Expert, Best Selling Author, Publisher, Speaker and Entrepreneur who helps WOMEN build successful and profitable businesses doing what they love.

She's a Certified Business, Life, Writing and PR Coach who teaches women a repeatable process and system for writing, launching, monetizing and scaling their business using a book.

Whether they're just starting out and writing their first book or they're looking to scale to 7 Figures and beyond. Charlotte has the knowledge, tools and experience you need to take your business to the next level! Her ultimate goal is helping more women work SMARTER not harder while creating more FREEDOM.

Her journey from working as a full-time licensed hairstylist employee to becoming a successful entrepreneur has inspired more than 5000 women globally to build their own businesses. She dedicates this chapter to you and her mom Sylinda Simon Shirer who died from cancer in May of 2017. Charlotte's mom was the #firstlady who introduced her to the Wealthy Women Lifestyle.

Wealthy Women Lifestyle

by Charlotte Howard Collins

Are you ready to kiss the fears keeping you from stepping into the role of a successful Mompreneur goodbye?

Let's just get right into it. If right now you're...

- Stuck in the day-to-day minutiae of running your business such as reading and sending way-too-many invoices, managing a busy inbox and fixing tech issues left and right!

- Feeling overwhelmed by everything on your plate, from client work to the marketing who knew a 15 minute video could take so long to make!

- Not outsourcing or handing off tasks that allow you to stay in your Zone of Genius!

- Just doing your best to get through each day without a meltdown, rather than focusing on projects that will move your business forward!

- Viewing your business as your whole source of identity and therefore taking everything personally!

- Implementing old ideas vs. brainstorming new ideas which is— let's be honest—your favorite thing to do!

- Allowing any and everything to affect how you show up in your business, doubting your decisions, wondering if you're "worth it" and negatively comparing yourself to every shiny Mompreneur out there with a filtered selfie and a post about their latest 6-figure launch which seems to be every single one of them!

Oh my goodness, I have been there too!! But I've got some not-so-great news: You might be running a business, but you're not operating like a successful Mompreneur should.

No wonder your business feels like it's running you, instead of the other way around! Now don't get me wrong: I get it. I am a loving wife and Mompreneur with four beautiful kids. I love my family with all my heart and have more than five businesses I love with all my heart too but sometimes things don't go as planned. Odds are, you created your business because you had a big, audacious goal or dream. You had a vision. Hopefully you still do!

But then something happened: You tried to bring that vision to fruition and discovered it's actually not as easy as that beautifully-written Facebook ad from that beautifully-dressed influencer made it seem.

Maybe you started pouring all your time and energy into Instagram Reels because another Mompreneur swore it worked for her, but didn't see a single sale after months and months of awkward dancing on camera.

Maybe you tried to outsource once or twice, but didn't love the results and decided, "Forget it. I might as well do it myself."

Or maybe you put every ounce of energy you had into a course or program and put it out there with bated breath but didn't see even a single sale in your early bird window, so you decided to scrap the whole thing.

Sound about right?

I won't lie to you: Managing a business as a Mompreneur isn't easy. It will force you to face every negative thought, belief and worry you've ever had about yourself and your abilities.

It'll push you to your edge, make you question your every move and if you're doing it "right," it will absolutely make you wonder whether you're really cut out for this whole "running a company" thing (more than once!).

Running a company can break you down...if you let it.

The good news is you can change all of that–with a little help.

There's a Reason Why Some Mompreneurs Crush It Online But It's Probably Not What You Think!

Here's the deal: You know other Mompreneurs maybe even Mompreneurs who are less talented and less tech-savvy than you are, who make this whole business thing work–and work well.

The good news is truly successful Mompreneurs aren't these fearless, *un*-human beings.

Being a "SUCCESSFUL" Mompreneur doesn't require joining the 5 a.m. club, taking cold showers to jolt your system 3x a day or spending hours on a cute meditation cushion to the point that your butt goes numb. Although you've probably been told all these things–and lots more! –is required.

Truly successful Mompreneurs like all of the moms in this book are just better at managing the mess inside their minds.

Instead of giving into their fears and doubts, they've learned to *transform* them.

They've learned to let go of their reservations around outsourcing. They don't even *try* to do it all, because they know they can't! They quiet the inner critic that tells them they're not good enough to lead or create or *whatever-else,* and they've done the work to confidently charge what their work is worth.

They've also learned to deeply trust their intuition, make decisions they believe in without mulling them over for years! They choose business strategies that feel right for them—not just following what every other glossy-Mompreneur-on-the-block is doing.

The better news is that YOU can learn how to do all of the above and more, too. It's time for you to become the CEO of your own life as a Mompreneur, Welcome to the Wealthy Women Lifestyle.

To live the Wealthy Women Lifestyle, you must:

Stop Thinking Like an Employee and Make Your Mompreneur Mindset Priority #1

Mindset is everything when it comes to running a successful business. I learned that from my mom. When you have the right mindset – often referred to as a growth mindset – you dream big and get excited about mapping out a business plan that will help you make those big dreams a reality.

You have a naturally positive attitude about your business and know in your heart that you WILL be successful; there are no "ifs" in this equation. Even though you don't know exactly what the road to success might look like, you are confident that you'll reach those big goals.

Determine if you're thinking like a Mompreneur or an employee, here are a few simple ways to decipher which one you are right now.

- **If you're already viewing your business like a Mompreneur, you're:**

  – Vision-driven

  – Able to outsource without fear or your own ego getting in the way

- Able to "disconnect" emotionally and not take things in business personally

- Working on projects that will build or scale your business regularly

- Taking regular time outs to work ON your business and brainstorm ideas for new projects, products, services, etc.

- Being a leader – embodying the qualities and values you preach, stepping into new territory regularly, expressing your truth without fear

- **If you're thinking like an employee, you're more likely to spend your days:**

  - Stuck in the day-to-day minutiae of running your business (admin work, tasks outside your zone of genius)

  - Feeling overwhelmed by everything on your plate

  - Not outsourcing or handing off tasks that allow you to stay in your Zone of Genius

  - Just doing your best to get through each day rather than focusing your time on projects that will move your business forward

  - Viewing your business as your whole source of identity and therefore taking everything personally

  - Implementing old ideas vs. brainstorming new ideas

  - And most importantly: Living from a place of fear – letting your own personal "stuff" stop you from moving toward the goals, dreams, and vision you once had for your business and life

I would love to help you implement all of this and help you make your dreams a reality. Join my FREE Facebook community at www.WealthyWomenInnerCircle.club

Nicole Curtis

She Rises Studios Senior Recruitment and Sponsorship Sales Manager

https://www.linkedin.com/company/she-rises-studios
https://www.instagram.com/sherisesstudios
https://www.facebook.com/sherisesstudios
https://www.sherisesstudios.com
https://www.facebook.com/groups/sherisesstudioscommunity

Speaker, Author, Leader. Nicole is a much sought-after expert with over 13 years of combined experience in Personal Growth and Self-Leadership which helped her overcome childhood sexual abuse, binge eating and break free from toxic relationships. She is a Mental Health Advocate for moms that have children who are struggling and she is on a mission to make sure that "no mom" feels alone in their journey of helping their child. Nicole founded Kapow Media LLC in 2018 and more recently became the Senior Recruitment and Sponsorship Sales Manager at She Rises Studios. Nicole inspires and empowers womenpreneurs all around the world and she loves to help them get their business visible worldwide.

Unstoppable Big Girl Pants

by Nicole Curtis

Being a Mompreneur is a lot like riding a rollercoaster!

One moment you feel like you're on top of the world, the next moment you can't shake the feeling of uncertainty and the fear of falling.

You experience both exciting and thrilling moments, but you also experience ups and downs, twists and turns, and bumps while on the ride.

I can't speak for you, but my Mompreneur journey has been filled with all of the above.

I have moments when I find myself struggling to find stability between being a mom and owning a company. I love being a mom, but I also love my work. It is easy for me to get sucked into the cycles of working more and mothering less, or mothering more and working less. I think this happens to many of us who are both moms and entrepreneurs. The pull we feel between the two can be overwhelming and sometimes frightening.

We don't want to be seen as the mom that loves her work more than her kids. The pressure is real that if you spend too much time at work, people will think that you are a bad mom or that your priorities are upside down, or if you spend all your time with your kids, you think that your work is going to suffer and fall apart.

I have battled with this instability quite often and what I have found to be true is that one, all that I do in my work is to be an example to my kids. To show them what working from purpose and passion looks like. Two, when I'm spending time with my kiddos, my company isn't going to suffer or fall apart. One of the reasons I became an entrepreneur was to buy back my time. To spend it how I wanted to. There is no need to feel guilty about this.

We all have those days where we will be head over heels in love with raising our kiddos. We will also have days where we are head over heels in love with our work, and that is ok. There's plenty of love to go around!

As I'm writing this to you, I have two teenagers living at home. Yes, I am in the middle stages of motherhood where I still have two children, but before I know it, they will both become adults. Ahh, I am so not ready for this!!

My oldest is a beautiful, strong-willed sixteen-year-old young lady who at times knows everything. I cannot fault her for thinking this way. I remember being that age and thinking the same way, and my youngest is a handsome, compassionate thirteen-year-old boy who likes to keep the peace.

My daughter is creative, intelligent, and loves a good adventure, and my son is entertaining, detailed, and lives life cautiously. Both of my kiddos are incredible humans and they equally bring me so much love, joy, and fulfillment as a mother. They complete me in so many ways. There isn't a day that goes by that I don't thank God for choosing me to be their mother and for giving me these two wonderful blessings in my life to raise and love.

Outside of being a mother, I am an entrepreneur, which God has given me another calling in my life to serve, love, and support women all over the world. Every day, I am grateful to have been given this mission because it brings me so much joy, light, and meaning in my life.

Being a Mompreneur is one of the greatest blessings in my life, especially during the blissful moments, but what do you do when hard and heavy moments hit?

It can become easy to let uncertainty and fear set in and start questioning yourself as a Mompreneur.

Questions like

"What if I mess up?"

"What if I'm making a big mistake?"

"I can't do this?"

"How am I going to manage this all?"

It's almost like you're screaming, "Stop the ride, I want to get off. This isn't what I thought it was going to be like.

When the questioning starts, it is very crucial that you don't let your critical voice derail you!

Don't believe for a second that you are unworthy or incapable of being a great mom and an entrepreneur. You can be both!

There are moments where I have questioned my ability to either continue on the Mompreneur ride or get off.

As a mother and as an entrepreneur, I believe that when the hard and heavy moments hit in life, it is a good time to see them as life lessons.

How I like to look at it is that you can either let life happen to you or for you.

You can either let circumstances or events in your life break you or you can see them for what they are, no matter how painful or hard they are, and learn something from them to become a better you.

So where do you go from here? Well, if you want life to happen for you, how I do it is I lean into a whole lot of faith, self-love and coffee, along with wearing my unstoppable big girl pants.

As a Mompreneur, you are going to experience some very hard and heavy moments. You are going to question yourself and it is certain that some kind of worry, doubt, and fear is going to creep in.

When these moments happen it is perfectly ok, and if you need to go right ahead and throw a little temper tantrum. Life is hard. Feel free to kick, scream, and ugly cry all you want, mama! Just promise me that you will not stay in this place. The place of feeling defeated and hopeless.

No! No!

Don't quit, cave in, hide, or give up!

You are an UNSTOPPABLE MOMPRENEUR!!

Get back up, wipe away those tears of despair, adjust your messy bun, put on some lipstick and charge forward wearing those Unstoppable Big Girl Pants.

No matter what life throws at you, wearing your Unstoppable Big Girl Pants will give you power to help you fight during the "I don't know if I can survive this" and the "oh my, I'm not sure about this" kinds of moments.

If you need a pair, it's ok hun, here you can borrow mine, or if you want your own pair, below is a list showing you what my unstoppable big girl pants are made of.

FAITH,

BELIEF,

SELF-TRUST,

UNSTOPPABLE MINDSET,

RELENTLESSNESS

When I walk into each day wearing my Unstoppable Big Girl pants, it is when I become my most powerful self!

Walking in FAITH that I am never alone, that God is always fighting right beside me. Having BELIEF that I can do anything I put my mind to. SELF-TRUST makes me able to overcome and conquer whatever comes my way. It gives me the strength to continue on my ride and the courage to get back up when I feel like I'm falling. An UNSTOPPABLE MINDSET allows me to choose and decide who I am becoming and that I am worthy of it. I am a brave, bold and determined woman! RELENTLESSNESS gives me the strength to keep moving forward and to never give up. That I can say yes to being fully me and that that is enough. I am fierce and I will fight to be the best mom and entrepreneur I can be.

I can't tell you how many times while wearing my Unstoppable Big Girl Pants I have been able to overcome and conquer unthinkable moments in my life as well as walk through the unknowns in life.

My hope for you is that when you are wearing your unstoppable big girl pants, you too feel like your most powerful self and that you can overcome and conquer any hard and heavy moment that hits you because you are not just powerful, you are a beautiful woman, an amazing mom, and a kick butt entrepreneur!

You are An Unstoppable Woman Mompreneur!!

Michèle Kline

Kline Hospitality Consulting LLC

http://www.linkedin.com/in/michelekline
http://www.instagram.com/micheleklinekhc
https://www.facebook.com/klinehospitalityconsulting
http://www.klinehospitality.com

Through intentionality and dedication, Argentinean immigrant Michèle Kline, built a career in the Hospitality Industry "playing chess and not checkers". In 2005 she became a Mother and soon after founded Kline Hospitality. As a high-achieving Woman, what propelled her to open her business was an unparalleled passion to strengthen operating procedures, enhance company culture, focus on leadership development; and above all, break the glass ceiling, excel as a Leader and be a Mom; ALL at the same time.

As a certified Coach and Process Improvement expert, she is known for genuinely caring about her client's growth. As an industry expert, she provides Organizational Effectiveness Coaching and Executive Coaching with her special ingredient, passion. Received the 2018 Hospitality Learning & Development Professional of the Year award in Nevada, and in 2021, honored among the 15 Top Hospitality Trainers globally.

A devoted Wife and Mother of three loving, witty, inquisitive children.

Unconditional LOVE always WINS!

by Michèle Kline

Dear Reader,

In case we haven't met before *(go read the first two books, for context and some laughs… just saying)*, my name is Michèle and I am a quiet and humble Ninja Warrior of my own life. An introvert, a high-achieving businesswoman, a Mom.

In 2005 I fell in love, a kind of love so deep, I didn't even think I could EVER love this way.

With the birth of my first son, I realized that there is nothing as powerful as a mother's love and nothing as healing as her child's smile or laughter.

There are many stories I can share with you today that are a testament of what unconditional love means to me. Like, my heart "bleeding pain" as I desired to have more kids and did EVERYTHING possible to make that dream my reality. Or the times I had to take drastic action, in situations I became aware I was not intentionally present. But, for the sake of word-count and not getting "too emotional", I am going to share the story of when I traveled across the state with Bob Marley, Madonna, The Rolling Stones, Coldplay and Blondie.

(screech sound) **Wait what?!** This is the moment the roller coaster starts heading up, and you anticipate what is coming next with fear, anxiety and a hint of excitement.

I caught your attention now, didn't I?

Okay, here we go; double-check your buckle, keep your hands inside the cart because you are about to take the ride of your life!

Grab a notepad, a pen and pay attention as we ride through the tools of what makes me an Unstoppable Mompreneur.

As my business started expanding, I started traveling quite a bit. One Sunday night, when putting my little boy to bed, he looked at me with deep sorrow in his eyes and softly asked: "do you **really** have to go Mommy?" My heart dropped.

I was in the middle of a takeover, and my presence during that trip was crucial to my client, their client, my business, and quite frankly, to me.

I knew he had a decisive soccer match that Saturday. With conviction, I looked intensely into his eyes and spoke to his soul, "I promise I will be back on Friday." Little did I know that a terrific wind storm was coming to Reno.

I counted the days to get back home. I called every evening and discussed the upcoming soccer match. I wanted us to have something we both looked forward to sharing. I longed to fill the void; perhaps I desired to ease my feeling of guilt.

I was anticipating my return after an exhausting but successful week. When I arrived at the airport that evening, it was closed. CLOSED?!?!?! Nooooo. By no means could planes depart in that storm. I checked the weather online in hopes that I could fly out the next day. Instantly, my kid's words resonated in my brain, followed by my promise of being home by Friday.

I had promised I would be there Friday!

So, without hesitation, I ran like a maniac to the rental car booth, assuming I had to beat everyone else. (Picture the 1990's movie Home Alone, when the Family is trying to catch their flight and Chuck Berry's "Run Rudolph Run" is playing in the background).

I rented a car. Success!

When I finally got in my rental, I felt a sense of victory, yet a colossal fear overtook me. I was about to drive across the state ALL BY MYSELF, tired and at night.

Now, this may sound silly to most but to me, it was a pivoting moment. A moment of growth, a moment when I realized I AM unstoppable and I WILL get home to my baby on time. I buckled up, adjusted my seat and mirrors, and plugged my phone into the vehicle's audio system.

THIS was going to be a ride to remember.

I was determined. I was on a mission! I looked through the rear-view mirror as the city was becoming smaller and smaller until it hid behind the mountain, and it was game on. I invited all the artists I mentioned above to my ride, and we had a blast. I sang loud to every tune and embraced that moment of growth with every sense, 451 miles across the desert, with NOTHING around. L-I-T-E-R-A-L-L-Y.

I stopped once because my bladder was giving up, and my vehicle needed fuel. Honestly, I feared for my life. The gas station was sketchy, as were the people in it. Then, I drove and drove and drove for a total of 7.5 hours, non-stop.

Since then, I have created more opportunities to grow like this one, and be an unstoppable Mom, because I can!

These, my friend, are some of the tips I can give you so that you stop feeling guilty, start patting yourself on the back and feel empowered. Because no matter what, unconditional LOVE always WINS!

⚒ **Stop. Breathe. Regroup.** It is very easy to get into a never-ending hamster wheel, when you are career-oriented. That is not healthy for your business, your kids, your partner or yourself. When you feel that way, take a deep breath and revisit where you are standing. Figure out if there is anything you can delegate or condense from your never-ending "to do" list and regroup.

✂ **Lean in.** Select your Board of Directors: those people in your life who you can trust for advice, help, feedback, and a sanity-check here and there.

✂ **Squash comparison.** You are unique. Do you hear me? So, stop comparing yourself to other Moms. Your Family's dynamics and values are different. So why would you compare yourself and your children to others, CONSTANTLY!?

✂ **Stop trying to be perfect.** Choose what works for your family. For example, nutrition and exercise are crucial to me. The kids may have a messy room, and laundry may be piling. However, I assure the kids play in the sun and have a healthy homemade meal. There are days when I cannot keep all my ducks in a row. I choose what works for the kids and me; I prioritize if I have to.

✂ **Normalize shared household duties.** Wake up! This is the 21st century. It is TOTALLY ok to split responsibilities at home. My husband has always been a big supporter of my career, and I couldn't do it if I had to do it all. Find what feels "heavy" to you and see if your partner or someone around you, can take the lead. My husband and I support the idea that a "real" Woman can do anything herself, but a "real" Man wouldn't let her. Divide and conquer!

✂ **Be present.** Be intentional with the time you spend with your kids. Would you dare look at your phone or watch while sitting with a client, an employee or a co-worker? No. Schedule time with your kid, put your phone down and be present, with every sense in your body, and give them your all! It is better to have *quality* time than to have *unintentional* time.

⚒ **The best you can.** Kids do the best they can with the capabilities, knowledge and tools they have. So do parents. Remember this! Stop beating yourself up for what you did or didn't do. You are not a bad parent, they are not a bad kid. Repeat to yourself out loud: *"I'm doing the best that I can!"*

⚒ **Have fun.** Our responsibilities sometimes feel like they are written on an endless ancient scroll. Make time to have fun. Find fun things to do WITH your kid(s), things you both enjoy. Have a dance party in their room right before bed, play question games during dinner time, go for bike rides. As a Mom of boys, I can tell you that it is not always easy to find common ground, but we make it work. You can do it too.

⚒ **Put your mask on first.** You know how flight attendants remind adults who travel with kids, to put their mask on first on the plane should it go down? Same concept. I truly admire my husband for this. He knows that he can serve others better, when he is 100% himself. This is one of the skills that makes him an unstoppable Dad. Grab a bite when you are hungry. Rest when you are tired. Take that bubble bath when you need to decompress. Step away from EVERYTHING else. It is a game changer when you start practicing this! You will be a much better person when you satisfy your most basic needs. STOP putting yourself last!

Whether you are a Mompreneur, a Momployee or a care-giver, your time with that child is critical to their development. Do the best you can, remember your actions are coming from your heart, and know that whatever it takes, in the end, unconditional LOVE always WINS!

Natalie Pickett

Entrepreneur, Speaker and Mentor

https://www.linkedin.com/in/natalie-pickett-74b00910
https://www.instagram.com/natalie_Pickett_Mentor/
https://www.facebook.com/nataliepickettmentor
http://www.nataliepickettmentor.com
https://www.facebook.com/groups/livingthedreamcommunity

Natalie Pickett is an award-winning business leader and much sought-after business mentor and speaker. An international best-selling author, Natalie has been featured in major news publications in Australia and the USA. An entrepreneur for 30 years, she is founder of multiple successful businesses. In this book Natalie demonstrates how she adapted her life after the birth of her daughter Jasmine (now 20) and generously shares insights into her triumphs and so called 'failures' as a Mompreneur with a multiple 7 figure business, ultimately discovering that success is less about hard work and more about finding joy.

It is possible to define your own version of success and easily take the steps you need to achieve your goals. It is possible to not just 'Dream the Dream' but 'Live the Dream'! Passionate about sharing this with the world, Natalie shows you how in her writing, speaking, mentoring and her online courses.

Is it possible to 'live the dream'?

by Natalie Pickett

'Living the dream' is one of my mottos. It is possible to create the life you want, the freedom to choose how you spend your time, the income you want, and feel fulfilled in your daily life. As a serial Mompreneur, I've discovered that becoming unstoppable is less about hard work and more about finding joy in every day. All my businesses come from my passions, and as a business mentor and speaker for over 12 years, I share this knowledge and help others take their business and daily life from surviving to thriving.

Travel is a big part of my life, and at 28 years old, I established my first business — an inbound travel company bringing international visitors to Australia. I grew this business to multiple 7 figures, and for 15 years I steered it through disruptions including natural disasters, pandemics and acts of terrorism. There were also internal challenges, especially when, as a mother, I needed to juggle many conflicting demands.

When my daughter Jasmine was born, my business was in a major growth phase. I already had a lot of procedures in place, but growing a team needs to come from a collective. If it is only you driving your business, it won't work without you. I wanted time off and had established systems to check in by working remotely and coming into the office once a week, leaving the day-to-day operations to my team. From the time she was 8 weeks old, Jasmine travelled with me on business trips around the country. She wouldn't take a bottle, so I needed to make time in my schedule to feed her.

One of the biggest challenges was my expectations of how much I could achieve in a day. Your time is no longer your own, and your baby's needs will dictate the schedule. You can do it all, just not all at once!

I was often in business meetings with my daughter. One memorable occasion involved her ballet school's strict rules about 'proper' ballet buns. My husband was to take her to class but couldn't manage the bun, so he dropped by the office. Whilst meeting with one of our key suppliers, I completed the bun AND a successful multiple-figure negotiation. Some days, it all works!

To help grow and scale, I decided to employ a General Manager. Anyone who has tried to replace themselves in their own business will know how challenging this is. You wear so many hats that it is difficult to find someone who can replace you.

At this level, you need to provide support, but also step aside so they can take ownership. Unfortunately, they weren't the right fit, and I realize that I should have made the decision to cut them loose earlier, but I really wanted this handover to work, so I was slow to let them go. I was also considering selling the business, but when the 2007–2008 Global Financial Crisis hit, selling an international travel business was unlikely.

This 'crash' was certainly a crisis, but it was also an opportunity to create the life I really wanted. I had let my business take over my needs, and it was now time to close it. I am thankful for the lessons learned, and I use that experience when helping clients create resilient businesses that support their needs and desires.

Mompreneurs are not only scrutinized and judged on how well we are managing motherhood, but also our businesses. Everyone has an opinion, and we are subjected to conflicting advice daily.

Closing my business also created a huge identity shift. When you attach who you are to what you do and how well you do it, what happens when you don't do it anymore? I was also going through a difficult divorce involving financial and custody disputes. As much as this was a crisis, when I lost everything, I became rich overnight because I realized that I hadn't lost the things that were important to me. Jasmine and I were safe and well.

The 'light bulb' moment was that I was prioritizing everyone and everything but myself. I realized it's not selfish to make time for yourself. I manifested a new dream life, a dream home, and a 6-figure consulting, speaking, and mentoring business. I worked part-time hours, prioritizing myself and time with Jasmine.

Doing lots of things for others is a mom's daily routine – add a business on top, and it is easy to forget about you. There is often guilt associated with taking time for yourself; "I should be spending time with my daughter" or "I should be working on my business", which eats away at any leisure time you might have.

Our energy is a resource, and if we constantly give, eventually it will deplete – and the pattern of giving more than we get back will eventually take its toll. This manifests as exhaustion, illness, and depression, and the only person who can make time for you is you.

My top 5 tips for successful Mompreneurs:

1. **Prioritize yourself** - when Jasmine was young, I struggled with making time for myself, but if I wasn't making myself a priority, how could I expect others to make me one? I realized the best example I could set for my beautiful daughter was a happy mom who knew how to look after herself. I was independent and capable, but I had not been nurturing myself. In one of my workshops, we explore core values and their integration into decision making – and the process for decision making is always YOU first. Ask yourself, "Is this okay with me?" and then consider

how it affects others. If it's not okay with you, then it's not okay. Learning to say "No" in this considered way is very empowering.

2. **Good foundations** – these consist of systems and structures, but they also include knowing how to support yourself, building a good support team, and asking for help when you need it. You might be able to do all the things in your business, but if you want to scale, you need to bring in team members, for whom you need systems and procedures. Just like buildings, businesses need strong foundations.

3. **Emotional intelligence** – being an observer of your emotions and understanding why you are experiencing them and using them to guide you to what you need to do next.

   People separate 'business' from 'personal', but this is never entirely true. Everything is personal because we are human beings, and as Mompreneurs this is an advantage. Tapping into our EI, we don't take the 'top down' authoritarian approach and we stand out as evolved leaders. I learned that there is strength within vulnerability, and that I needed to trust myself and let go of fears around emotions, make decisions with an open heart, be guided by my intuition, and prioritize my own needs. These were key steps to creating my dream life.

4. **Manage your energy** — one of the most important resources is your energy. Knowing how to read your energy, and that of others, is crucial. For Mompreneurs, this is amplified. Failure to take time to restore your energy will lead to burnout. If you are experiencing fatigue, resistance, or frustration, reset and restore your energy until you can move forward from a place of inspiration.

5. **Know your value** — this can be achieved by aligning to your value set and operating from there. As Mompreneurs we often

undervalue what we do. A key decision for me when launching my consulting business was to charge based on the value I brought to my clients, which was more than others were charging. I had a unique skill set and experience that had taken years to develop. Someone told me I should charge less so I could get more work. I decided that would mean that I was working more to achieve less. Charge your value so you have quality time for clients and your personal life. When you operate from a place of value, you eliminate self-doubt and align with your sense of purpose, and you are less likely to be affected by any negativity.

Aligning with your values is also a way to restore energy. This topic is one of my most popular workshops — creating a Company Culture with shared goals will engage your staff and attract customers who align with a business that shares similar values to them. When we are working with people who align with our values, we are following our joy.

Our businesses should work for us, not the other way around. The key to success is creating a business that has the momentum to work without you. My biggest takeaway is to not put off living your dream life while waiting for something to happen in the future. Enjoy each of the steps along the way, and don't try to do everything at once. If business becomes stressful, remind yourself of what is important to you, and that business and life are supposed to be fun.

Alyson MacLeod

Soul Expression Sessions
Founder & CSO (Chief Soul Officer)

https://www.linkedin.com/in/alyson-m-macleod-25111a9
https://www.instagram.com/alyson_macleod
https://www.facebook.com/alyson.macleod1
www.soulexpressionsessions.com

Alyson MacLeod, CHC is a best selling author, speaker, serial entrepreneur, podcast host and Transformational Results Coach certified in Health, Life and Business Coaching. She has a degree from Algoma University in Community, Economics, and Social Development. Alyson coaches Executive and high achieving Entrepreneurial Women who have lost their drive to succeed in life, find happiness, passion and confidence again to Live the Life of their Dreams. They refocus, gaining clarity and learn to live in their full Soul Expression as God intended using her Soulful Living Blueprint. Alyson's inspirational podcast, magazine and tv show called Soul Expression Sessions are hosted on the Wealthy Women's Entrepreneurial Network.

Somersaults and Power Rangers
Along for the Ride!

by Alyson MacLeod

So, what do you do when you find yourself 12 weeks pregnant with your second child after you were told you were never going to be able to conceive and you just finished a custom built 3 bedroom house, and one of those bedrooms is your office?

Luckily for me my first born, Maxwell, was always along for the ride. He was actually over the moon excited that he could share my office with me as his bedroom. I was lucky to get the entire power rangers station and patrol to watch over me every day, perched on the end of my 9' long executive desk with guns ready just in case the printer or any other technology decided to act up. Such a blessing!!

It was a fun time but also a challenging one. I had a newborn and a 6 year old both vying for my attention. Some days it was Keegan in the swing and Maxwell in front of the TV. The biggest lesson learned was that flexibility in all things was the key.

"There is no way to be a perfect mom,
but a million ways to be a good one!"
Jill Montgomery

As a mompreneur it was always my intention to include my child (and now children) on the entrepreneurs journey. I was blessed to be able to bounce back and forth between executive jobs and entrepreneurship for 15 years. It was March 1, 2001 and Keegan was 8 days away from arrival! I was the Regional Channels Manager for Terradata for Canada and even pregnant I was on the road 3-4 days a week up until the last weeks before Keegan's birth.

My technical team thought I was crazy and being all men I never had to carry a thing (none of their wives had children yet and fragile was an understatement - them I mean!). If I was close to home, Maxwell got to come along for the ride. He loved helping me set up for presentations and knew it better than I did some days.

Once Keegan arrived and I was on maternity leave, we spent more time together at parks, zoos and beaches. I was enjoying being with my children and the other mothers in the neighborhood. I remember 9/11 well. I was taking my car in to get it serviced and Keegan was fast asleep in the back car seat and Maxwell was at school. Every radio station was in panic mode and I could not understand what was happening. When I brought Keegan into the waiting room everyone's eyes were glued to the TV. It was devastating and I sat him down quietly and cried with everyone in the room. I had friends in the towers and felt numb. All I could do was hope and pray they were ok.

As a mother, in that moment, I never wanted to leave my children ever again. It was scary to think that this can happen so close to home with people who lived just down the block from us. Two days later we received word that they were not in the buildings at the time but out on the street. Hearing the stories of them running for their lives was heart wrenching. Life changed for all of us that day. I was about to go back to work early from maternity leave but there was such a shift in our business that I had no resellers to manage any longer. Overnight, 38 resellers across Canada were gone. I did not have a job to go back to so I had to pivot.

I started looking for a job but they only hired ex IBM managers with 40 years experience to do what I could so I pivoted again and decided that I was going to be an entrepreneur again. It was easy to come up with what I loved to do outside of work but not sure on the how. I was a self-professed workout junkie. When we were traveling selling software, we would be in the gym in the morning and if we had a rough day we were in the gym at night, so it only made sense to do something in the health and wellness field.

I went to a Curves and to an independent gym to see what they had to offer. I could not get a Curves Franchise but an older lady overheard my conversation with the owner and told me to go online and source my own equipment. So, I did just that and Canadian Woman's Fitness was born. We moved to Kingston from Toronto and opened 2 gym locations in 5 months. It was exciting and a huge family affair. My husband and I did about 85% of the construction work and the in-laws were able to help with the kiddos when they couldn't join in.

Maxwell would help paint the bottom part of the walls and my husband Michael painted the rest. Keegan just got dirty doing somersaults all over the place and loved every second of it. Once the water bottles came in, Maxwell placed them perfectly in each of the cubicles and Keegan would knock them down. I still remember the laughter and screams which made the entire adventure worthwhile. As a mom that made my day. It was that my little humans could get the biggest joy out of the little things with us as we built our future business together, as a family.

When we opened the doors in April 2003 at the first location, Maxwell was there to help with the tours and handing everyone a water bottle. He was my VIP and a huge part of what was happening. He needed to know it was hard work but it was also extremely rewarding. He was also happy to leave Keegan with Grandma for the day and be in charge like a big boy! When he thanked me at the end of the day for a job well done, I was in tears. I will never forget that feeling of joy that being with my children through this journey brought to my life.

In August 2003 we opened the second location and there was a daycare right next door which was super convenient for Keegan to attend. Maxwell was in school and we were seemingly making inroads, making money and having fun with this great venture. Things got very efficient and systemized as the business grew and there were times that each child could come with me to work and say hi to the ladies. Maxwell was on the weekends and helped to organize my office and Keegan was during the week when I had shopping and paperwork to do. That way they could each feel special on their own days and they really felt like the gyms were a part of them too.

The gyms were sold in 2007 and a divorce shortly ensued, I moved back up north to Sault Ste Marie, Ontario with my kiddos. One of the biggest lessons I learned moving to my hometown is that listening to everyone else's idea of what I needed to do outweighed my desire to be an entrepreneur. It was that I was a single mom now and needed a "real job" and for a couple years I did just that. I was good at it but definitely not fulfilled by any means. I finally got hurt on the job and the employer did not own up to it so that was a 6 year ride of insanity. Once that was done and my self-esteem was about the lowest it ever could get, my son Maxwell told me, "I guess you just have to work for yourself again mom". How did I get such wise children? They both agreed and I dove back into entrepreneurship and never looked back!

The one thing I know about being an entrepreneur is that flexibility is #1. As I said earlier I learned a lot about flexibility being a mompreneur and the impact it would have on my children. The second biggest lesson learned was that I needed to be a constant and never-ending personal development student. I went on to be a certified Life, Business and Health & Wellness Coach rounding out my education with a degree in Community Economics and Social Development (graduating class - June 2022)!

My children now have aspirations of entrepreneurship and I cannot wait to see where it takes them. They both understand the complexities and they also have the knowledge and freedom to be who they need to be as an entrepreneur. They have learned from my mistakes and pitfalls. I never got into entrepreneurship to show them the way but it was to seek a better way for my family to navigate our lives together. I loved every second of it and still do!! I know that Maxwell and Keegan will always be my biggest cheering section and I will be theirs too.

After all, we are all along for the ride!!

Blessings!!

XOXOXO

Lovely LaGuerre

Founder Pure Heavenly Hair Boutique
Serial Entrepreneur and International Bestselling Author

https://www.instagram.com/pureheavenlyhair
www.LovelyInspireYou.com
www.PureHeavenlyHair.com

Lovely LaGuerre is a Serial Entrepreneur and International Bestselling Author. She believes in the power of collaborating with other women and sees how it lends to the growth of all involved. You can see this through the books she has chosen to be a part of, including "The Successful Woman's Mindset: 21 Journeys to Success" and most recently, "Becoming an Unstoppable Woman". In "Becoming an Unstoppable Woman" she shares her story that will empower you, will inspire you, and will uplift you.

Lovely is a successful Commercial and Luxury Real Estate Agent. She is on a mission to help others turn their real estate investment dreams into a reality. She's also the Founder of Pure Heavenly Hair Boutique, a luxury beauty brand transforming, inspiring, and empowering women to unleash their beauty inside and out. Additionally, she's the host of "Motivation with Lovely," a new series dedicated to motivating and empowering women, through interviewing fellow female entrepreneurs. She is a member of NAIOP, CALV, NAR, GLVAR Association, Wealthy Women Inner Circle, and many more! She resides in Las Vegas with her loving family.

The Ultimate Boss Mom

by Lovely LaGuerre

"I am a woman, a mother, and an entrepreneur."

Every noun of this resounding reminder is as powerful as my intrinsic urge to break the shackles so tightly worn by society.

I am an adoring mother of two girls they are my driving force and my *raison d'etre.* They are charismatic, beautiful inside and out, and they are forgiving souls. My first had led me to places and events I never dreamt about. I found a passion in being a pageantry mom, a soccer mom, and the list goes on with after-school curriculums and weekend activities. Her lively persona humbles me to do more with life than idling away. Her new life journey has just begun. As I count my blessings, I am fully cognizant of the bigger picture. I am certain that the divine placed my second daughter in my lap with a bigger purpose. My little future CEO she says she is a legend already; I never doubt that. Since she came, I feel contented, fulfilled, and humble. She inspires me every day with her innocent curiosity and untiring zip and zest.

My journey, from a woman to a mompreneur, is a travail through audacity and assuages, boldness, and brashness, discomfort and diffidence, expectancy and excitement: and more importantly culminated in gratitude and gladness.

I am constantly pushed to be the best version of myself, and my two kids make sure that every version of mine is inclusive, vibrant, and resilient. I hope that one day I will fulfill the purpose of my being by empowering them to create their empire. Feeling blessed is an understatement. I am eternally grateful for them. They have genuinely changed my life, from making me realize motherhood is the most challenging but most rewarding job to helping me become a mompreneur and taught me to be fearless and trust my gut feelings and intuition while making decisions.

The mompreneur's journey has surely been rewarding. I am stronger for it. I know that I am not perfect, but I am perfectly me, who is good enough for my kids. I take on whatever comes my way with a sword in my arm because I am strong, determined, and a force to be reckoned with. That is something, I believe, we all have inside of us. It is just a matter of finding it and using it.

My life has been balancing running a motherly household and being the Ultimate Boss Mom. I have also had to make sure they are well-rounded and keeping a growth mindset. I have taught them to be creative and to express themselves.

As the quote goes, "The best way to find out what we truly need is to find out what we truly want." I believe that this is true for everyone, but especially for mompreneurs. We need to find our own path and be true to ourselves. Only then can we indeed be successful.

Life challenges are vast and varied, but I believe that the most important thing is to stay true to yourself. On one hand, you are a mother, and on the other hand, you are an entrepreneur.

There are times when it's hard to stay positive and motivated, but if you have a clear vision of what you want to achieve, it'll be easier to push through the tough times. When you're feeling down, remember why you're doing this and what your goal is. Stay strong and don't give up on yourself.

Life challenges can seem insurmountable, but it is important to remember that you can overcome anything that comes your way.

You are strong, you are resilient, and you can achieve great things. Never forget that.

These are not just suggestions; they are based on my very own personal experiences!

I still remember the day I became a mompreneur. It was one of the best days of my life. I felt like I could do anything and be everything. I was excited and scared all at the same time. I knew that I had to be strong and be there for my daughters, but I also knew that I could build an empire for them and set an example by being present and by loving them all at the same time.

This means that you may have it all by just believing in yourself; you should not be forced to make a choice, and you should know that everything is possible with a smart attitude.

I had my moments of uncertainty and perplexity, but I kept pushing through them with determination. I needed to remind myself that I was doing this for the sake of my family. I wanted to serve as a role model, demonstrating to them that they too could create a world of wonders. They needed to know that they could always count on me to be there for them no matter the circumstances. This experience has also given me a newfound appreciation for my daily life.

I wanted to be a good example of a strong, successful, and happy mother. I am proud to say that I have managed to do just that. From fighting for my children's future to embracing my beliefs and everything in between, I have grown immensely as a person and as a mother. My children are my world, and I would do anything for them. This is the real strength of mompreunerialism.

My mother used to tell me that the sky was the limit for my dreams. Now, I know that the sky is limitless. I believe that if we put our thoughts to it, we can all be successful and happy in our lives.

As the quote goes, "Your only limit is the size of your dreams." Keep dreaming big because big dreams do come true and I know that if you work hard enough, anything is possible.

It may seem easier said than done and that is quite true. Not everything is green pastures and blue skies. Not for me at least. However, I was never quite up. I confronted each difficulty head-on and overcame each one.

Once, I was so close to success, but I failed. I had to start all over again. It was one of the most challenging things I have ever had to do, but I did it. I started from scratch, and I made it.

You see, the challenges and obstacles are part of the journey. They make us who we are.

We mompreneurs are like rabbits who keep running even when we are tired. We are like warriors who never give up. We are strong and we are powerful. We are like the sun that shines even on the darkest days.

Any mother that feels stuck in the leverage of being an amazing mother should take a deep breath because you are not alone. You are a mompreneur, and you've got this. I know it's not easy being a mother and an entrepreneur, but it is possible. You can do it with your stains, your tears, and your sheer determination.

Our kids are watching us. They are learning from us. So, let's be the best example we can be. Let's show them they can do anything they set their minds to. Let's show them that they can be happy and prosperous.

Teach our kids to develop a growth mindset to have success in anything they do. Show them that they can be anything they want to be.

Whenever you feel like giving up, remember this. I took a deep breath and decided to keep going even when it was hard. I told myself, "You are a mompreneur, and you can do this." I looked my daughters in the eyes, and I kept going. You can do this too.

If you ever want to give up....

Remember the story of the mother who came so close to realizing her objectives but ultimately fell short of her goals and aspirations? She had to go back to the beginning and start all over again from the beginning. Even though it was one of the most difficult situations, it did not prevent her from accomplishing her heart's desires. In the beginning, she began at the very bottom and worked her way up, constructing a foundation from the ground up.

Remember the story of a woman facing many challenges? At the end, she uses them as an advantage, overcoming her aches and pains by drawing on them as a valuable lesson and applying them in other situations. As a result of these encounters, she was changed into a better and more confident person in the aftermath.

When considering giving up on your aspirations and goals, always remember that you are not alone in your thoughts and feelings. As a mompreneur, you have total control over your firm's operations. You should want to be a fearless mompreneur who never gives up on your goals and desires, and that is precisely what you should strive to be. Yes, you have the skills and talents essential to complete the task! Put on your cape and showcase your powers to the rest of the world. Be proud!

Mompreneurs, our world needs us! We are women who can lead the way, never give up in the face of adversity, and have the know-how to bring out the best in others. We are the role models for the next generation, and it is our responsibility to show them that it is never too late to learn, grow, and become better versions of ourselves. From boardrooms to living rooms, from Wall Street to Main Street, women are making their voices heard and their presence felt. We are the change-makers, doers, and dreamers and we are just getting started.

Society may want to stop us, but we will not be silenced. We will continue to fight for what is right, and we will continue to lead the way. We are the women of the world, and we will not be denied.

So, to all the mompreneurs out there, I say to you...

Becoming a mompreneur has been an ardent journey for me. I scaled my business to heights I never planned to, and I got to develop a more rewarding relationship with my kids. I had more to teach, more to nurture, and more to nourish than before. In a way, going the businesswoman way, I have enriched myself professionally and personally. Mompreneurs are like pioneers and overloads of startups. There is no fixed roadmap to raised kids or revenues while having kids, but we do figure it all out, don't we? So, own your story, be proud how far you've come, be the light, be true to yourself, and best of all be uniquely you and it's okay to celebrate YOU!

Best of luck! Go show the world what you've made of!

Alicia Marcos Birong

Owner and Program Creator at ChatterGirls and Guided Choices Inc.

https://www.linkedin.com/in/alicia-marcos-birong-4716177/
https://www.instagram.com/alicia_birong/
https://www.facebook.com/alicia.m.birong
https://www.guidedchoices.org
https://chattergirls.net

Alicia Marcos Birong is a pioneer in the field of child mindfulness, speaking on the same stages with Mother Teresa and Pope John Paul II.

As the founder of Guided Choices, Alicia's signature programs have gathered national attention for their transformative abilities of children.

ChatterGirls™ offers in-person, hands-on guidance for 8-14 year old girls. Pediatric Life Coaching™ instructs parents, teachers, and coaches how to effectively help children overcome their daily hurdles.

Alicia's best selling book "Changing the Chatter" assists young girls in developing life skills for becoming strong, confident women.

A recipient of McHenry County Hero's Award, Alicia's passion for empowering children is evident. With 25+ years of experience as a therapist, counselor, life coach, and hypnotherapist, Alicia shares her expertise with communities across the country. You may have seen her on national television or working alongside companies such as Coca-Cola, Girls Scouts of America, American Express, and the YWCA.

A Mother's Legacy

by Alicia Marcos Birong

This chapter is for my girls

Moms are special. They bring you into this world and give you the best of what they have. They teach you about life and love and help you raise your own family when the time comes. I came into this world and learned I would have to teach myself about life and love. My mother gave her best to her own traumas and psychiatric issues and wasn't able to invest much in me or my brother. Thankfully, over the years, I have been blessed with a tribe of women to come alongside me and my family and help me be the best mom I can be.

Looking back, I wanted to be a good mother. I wanted to love my children, teach them good manners and how to love and be loved well. In reality, I was a train wreck. I sometimes wonder how I ever managed to get on the mom train since I didn't have a good example from my own mother. I did, however, learn a lot about being a mom from my own children. They taught me valuable life lessons. I will continue to teach others today.

Most of my life, I worked in a male-dominated workplace. Back in the 80's and 90's, when I first started working, women were told who they could be and how much money they could make. Similarly, the church worked hard to limit what I was capable of becoming, injuring my faith in the process. From the time I was a little girl, well into my adult years, my identity was beat down into a box. I fought through many of these issues while raising my own children. I truly didn't believe my daughter saw a good role model in me. I thought she saw someone who was broken, living in a broken marriage. All I wanted for her was to become a strong and confident woman.

One of the biggest lessons my daughter taught me as a young mom was how NOT to be a pushover. She would call me out when I would hesitate to follow through on discipline and let others push me around. This is something I am still working hard to overcome to this day.

I have two children and two grandchildren. As an entrepreneur, I get to be more invested and involved in their lives than I was ever able to be when I worked in the corporate world.

My daughter and granddaughter are an amazing team. I see things in my granddaughter that I taught my daughter, and it makes me so happy to see the good I was able to do as a mom come full circle. I firmly believe it takes a village to raise children, and my daughter has had many amazing women in her life that helped raise her. I do take the credit for the importance of family and God in her life. She has been through the worst and the best with me. She is by my side no matter what I need, and she is doing a beautiful job teaching her daughter about life and love. For many years, it was just us. I've watched her become who she wanted to be; a woman who says what needs to be said, no matter how it's received.

A few years back, I talked with my daughter and told her I needed to spread my wings and go beyond coaching, therapy, and hypnotherapy. To see what I could do to make a bigger impact in this world. At the time, my granddaughter was 2, and I knew I wanted to leave her something bigger than just memories. I wanted to leave her a legacy she could pick up if she wanted and be proud of what her mother and I had achieved as women.

There are very few material things people give me in life that matter more than their value to me as a person. The value women have in this world and the hard seasons they have journeyed through is priceless to me. In my own life, I survived abuse, unfair wages, belittling, and depression. My life is now committed to helping women in the same places not only survive, but go on to thrive and become strong, whole women. To make a difference, we must help our daughters, granddaughters, and any other women we come across in our lives. With over 65 years of life experience, I understand the needs our daughters and granddaughters have. In order for our girls to stand strong in life, we need to teach them how to celebrate their uniqueness.

My journey as an entrepreneur began back in 2013. I took the lessons I learned from the women and children who touched my life and my own experiences as a mother and turned them into my current afterschool program, ChatterGirls. I researched the development stages for girls, ages 8–14. I listened to them talk about the thoughts that get stuck in their minds, the words that others speak over them, and the words they speak over themselves. The mind is the most important tool on the journey to loving our uniqueness.

Long before we as a society started talking about mindfulness, I was working to help reshape lives, young and old alike, by knowing and using mindfulness tools to back up the power in their minds. It is exciting to write books, programs, and co-author books with my daughter's ideas, guidance, and input as I walk down this new path to leaving a worthy legacy.

As an entrepreneur, I have surrounded myself with great women who challenge me, support me, and work alongside me. Some of us try to just pay the bills and wonder what comes next in life. Becoming an entrepreneur is not easy. I read about so many people who have "3 simple steps to becoming successful" when in reality it is your uniqueness that makes the difference in your story. My favorite part about my story so far is this: I thought everyone else had the answer to becoming who I wanted to be, but the reality is that I am the answer to becoming who I wanted to be. I had to learn to believe in myself and my program.

We have an obligation to our children and those who cross our paths to share our life lessons and failures. Even now, as you read this, I am helping you with my story and experiences. I have always looked at my clients as family. It's what I do as a mom. I help, encourage, teach, support, and show them the way to their own success. If you are an entrepreneur, you may just be the mother and mentor that someone needs right now.

Let's take a moment to thank all of the mom entrepreneurs who have gone before us. Let's celebrate the change they brought in for us and let's be thankful for the change we are bringing to this world for your own daughters and generations to come.

To all the mom entrepreneurs who paved a path in my life, thank you! Thank you for your love, support and for honoring my journey to my own success. I wouldn't be where I am today without you all!

Who will you share your legacy with?

Jennifer Cairns

Founder @ Lady Rebel Club®, Rebel Business Coach & Mentor @ Rebel Leader Institute™, Ambassador for Neurodiversity & Hidden Disabilities, Co-Founder of Redefined Workforce, 2x International Bestselling Author, Speaker and Mum

https://www.linkedin.com/mwlite/in/jennifer-cairns
https://www.instagram.com/lady.rebel.club
https://www.facebook.com/LadyRebelClub
www.ladyrebelclub.com
https://www.rebelleader.institute

Jennifer Cairns is an entrepreneur, advocate, and innovative leader specialising in igniting women*entrepreneurs and business leaders who are neurodiverse or who have hidden disabilities. After years of feeling forced to hide her own diversities and disabilities while running her businesses, Jennifer decided enough was enough.

She now shows others how to toss the cookie-cutter approaches and use their uniquity in a way that skyrockets their confidence and ignites their brand. She empowers leaders to grow a purposeful business that suits their life and definition of success without the overwhelm or feelings of having to be perfect or fake.

Jennifer loves the juggle of working from home and says, "Kids can be a glorious source of inspiration, fun and creativity in our businesses. It's an opportunity to spark your child's imagination, lift their confidence and to create memories that everyone will cherish.".

Jennifer lives in Northern Ireland with her husband, two sons and four-legged bestie.

Business That Bonds

by Jennifer Cairns

Like most things in life, business is a juggle. Yet if we are purposeful, we can use our business as a way of creating even deeper bonds and wonderful, meaningful memories with our kids. Our business can become a vehicle that we use to share gifts with our children, grandchildren, or other children in our lives, and we might receive a few surprise gifts in return.

Gifts I've Received

I have always wanted to have my own business, even before I ever knew what the word entrepreneur was. I was extremely blessed that throughout my youth, I spent a lot of time with my grandparents. I remember so clearly my Grandma and Grandpa Harper taking me down to their campground where I'd spend entire days happily cleaning the paddle boats with gramps in the warm sun, lifting leaves and rocks off of the putt-putt course.

I remember helping Grandma Harper run the little store, stocking shelves, and arranging the displays to help sell that week's special. Although the work was fun, I also remember long days, often falling asleep in the truck on the way home, with the scent of dirt and sun lingering on my clothes as I drifted off. I learned to use my imagination, use my initiative to complete tasks, and that fun things can also be things that take a lot of work, time, and effort, and that was ok.

Another memory I have is walking into my Grandma Williams' office, seeing her behind her desk, and thinking "whoa." She was and still is, a force to be reckoned with, though not in an aggressive or loud way. I remember her always being purposeful with what she did. She was kind yet strong and I remember admiring how so many people respected her.

She would let me do the filing, pull policies, type up notes, and even more as I got older. I remember coming home from summer visits with suitcases filled with office supplies! She would often ask me, "What are questions we need to ask a policyholder that you don't see on the form?". That was always a great question as I would ponder it for hours sometimes, keeping myself occupied as I would scribble out strange scenarios. I realised 15 years later that she showed me how to approach problems from different angles and never think inside the lines.

My grandparents gave me many incredible gifts that have stayed with me my entire life. They gave me their most precious gift, time. Plus, they encouraged me to have the self-belief that I could do absolutely anything, including running my own business, and they sparked ideas and opened the door to my imagination. From there, I flew.

Gifts That Keep on Giving

As children grow into adults, they can learn new skills and gain knowledge. What can be difficult to adapt as adults is imagination, deep-seated self-belief, and grit during all the craziness when you run a business. As life's waves come crashing with bills to pay, children to look after, homes to tidy, often our self-belief fades, our grit slips, and our imagination is boxed up and put up high on the shelf out of reach.

It's not easy to be an entrepreneur, as you know. There are days, weeks, months, and even years when it feels like running a business is a boxing session. You get punched, jabbed, and sometimes knocked for six. Yet, we do our best more often than not to get back up and go another round.

Although I received many gifts from my grandparents, the most precious of all is the bond I had with them. The special bond made over typewriters, paddle boats, and store shelves made me believe in myself and sparked my thoughts about running my own business from such a young age. That kind of bond helped shape a child and give her lasting gifts.

Gifts You Can Give

What's great is you can create similar unique bonds with your kids, grandkids, any kids you love and want to share your world with. Empower and inspire them in ways you can't even imagine. Give their ideas wings, and if they choose to fly and one day run their own business, encourage self-belief that they too can soar even when the road is bumpy.

Exhibit problem solving, thinking outside-the-box, persistence, imagination, and self-belief. Allow them to see you as the strong, courageous, determined, and talented human you are beyond the labels. Have essential quality time and also have some good, downright silly fun.

Here are some ideas and ways my boys have helped me in our businesses from time to time:

1. Have them take your photos versus you snapping those awkward selfies. Setting up a photoshoot is fun, and it gives you both a chance to get creative. I did a shoot once with my youngest that involved him throwing glitter at me during the shoot. He enjoyed it a little too much and I probably swallowed a ton of the stuff, yet it was completely worth it, and he still mentions the "glitter shoot" years later.

2. Let them help you with tech, whether it's setting up your YouTube, TikTok, or resizing your thumbnails with a handy app they like (Yes, my son has helped me with all this!). Kids are growing up with tech in a way we didn't. Let them practice showing their knowledge, adaptability, and leadership to those older than them. This impactful experience will help them greatly whether they work for themselves or others.

3. Let them help you come up with names for anything! Playing name games will grow their vocabulary and creativity. The more made-up the words are, the better.

4. Ask their opinion about your new logo, business cards, Instagram, and book. Especially as children get older and they want to do photoshoots, show you how to use that new shiny photo editing app, or play the name game, they will usually gladly give you their opinion. It's an opportunity to have conversations with them during years when sometimes conversations can be a little one-sided. It lets them see their opinion has value to you and that they should be confident to express it. Their unique perspective often allows us to see something in a new light.

5. If it is with your business, why not do a YouTube-type show with your kids. It doesn't need to be expensive or fake. Think of a theme that would be fun to do. Or ask your kids to interview you on different topics. If you're brave, you could do these live. Though you never know what kids will say, a video might be safer. ☺

Here are some additional quick-fire ideas for getting your kids involved:

- Have them transcribe or caption videos

- Show them how to design in Canva

- Have them brainstorm some blog ideas, funny jokes to tell, or ideas for posts
- Have them be your teleprompter and hold your cards when recording
- Ask them to survey family or friends
- Have them research something
- Get them to help you organise your office room, nook or table
- Have them tear words/letters out of newspapers and magazines to use for photoshoots and videos
- Let them do your make-up for a fun photo or video shoot
- Ask them to help you make deliveries if applicable
- Have them help you practice that speech or decorate your desk
- If you have a bricks and mortar business, they can help tidy up, stock shelves, or create a display
- Ask them to make you a paperclip or pen holder, I still have one my son made eight years ago!
- Ask them to make a lunch for the two of you to share

Wrapping It Up

You'll be surprised what YOU can gain from all these experiences. not just the unique relationship you can build with your child, but what you can learn from them and how they might even help your business grow. Children are open-minded, creative, and honest. They are incredible people to have around when you're growing a business!

Be open to learning from them. Use their inventiveness, imagination, and openness to fuel your passion, creativeness, and vision. The unique memories and bonds you'll each have from these lived experiences together within your business will be priceless for you both.

This chapter is dedicated to my Grandma Harper who passed away many years ago from Alzheimer's, Grandpa Harper who sadly passed this year just days before his 95th birthday and Grandma Williams who will be 93 this July 4th. Thank you for inspiring me as a child and giving me so many wonderful gifts and to my two boys, Dillon and Callum, for inspiring me each and every day in numerous ways both in life and business. 🖤

Heather Stokes

Wife, Mother, Homeschooler & Business Owner

https://www.linkedin.com/in/heather-stokes-benton-899624204/
https://www.instagram.com/heathersfinancialfocus/
https://www.facebook.com/financiallyfocusedfamilies
https://www.financialgps-hs.com

I am a wife, mother, homeschooler and business owner. I am a giver, a motivator, a developer and I do not except the answer no. I only see it as a challenge. My road to success has changed many times. Life has derailed my journey and I have built a new path each time.

I went to college for Forensic Psychology worked for multiple government agencies over the next eight years. When I met my husband he was a flight attendant and owned a limousine business. We lived a lavish life. 9/11 was our first major set back, three years later he suffered major injury and then pancreatic cancer at 40.

I could given up, but with three girls to depending on us that was not an option. I had to learn how to be creative with money. Now it is my mission to help others to go from surviving too thriving. Being a mother and running a business can feel overwhelming at times. I find the key to keeping it all together is balance.

Finding Balance

by Heather Stokes

As women, we wear many hats. Juggling becomes our art form. The first thing you must understand and give yourself credit; being a Mom is a full-time job. Being an entrepreneur is a full-time job. Being a Mompreneur is a feat. Many people have never heard of a "Mompreneur" before. Even few have dared to become one themselves. We're a somewhat rare breed, but that's just part of what makes us spectacular. The dictionary definition is, a mother who is busy raising a business and a family. The reality is being a Mompreneur is so much more than that. As a Mompreneur, your clients, your team, employees (if you have any), and their families are your family too. You are responsible for providing for your children, and for your work family and their children. Mompreneurs are very aware of our ever-expanding family headcount, and it pushes us to be at the top of our game. Not just for ourselves, but for everyone who's counting on us. I have three girls. My oldest is in her 20's. I currently have a preteen and a very rambunctious toddler. I've been an entrepreneur for almost five years. In that time, I've aged probably 10 but I have also gained wisdom on what you need to be successful as a Mompreneur. Here are some tips and tricks for aspiring and currently conquering Mompreneurs out there.

Acknowledge your strength

I often hear people say "I don't know how you do it". As Women, we possess unbelievable inner strength. When you become a mother, that strength becomes otherworldly. Everything changes; your *why changes*. We are hyper-aware of how we interact with the world, and how it affects our children. Our understanding gives us strength, and that strength is superhuman. It's arguably what gives us our competitive advantage, even as we fight against disadvantages like; sleep deprivation, extreme multitasking, burnout, and rising above in a man's world. Own that inner strength and use it to your advantage, because it is your advantage.

Take time for yourself

As a Mompreneur, it's not just rare to have "me" time, it's a nonexistent concept. At any moment of the day, there will be someone who needs you either your children, spouse, family, clients, employees, friends. Like I said, we wear many hats! No one can function without blocking off some time for themselves. Self-care is crucial, even if just 15 mins in the morning before anyone gets up. Succeeding in all roles depends on it. Mompreneurs are always running up against the clock, so you have to be strategic with your time. Always be on the lookout for ways your time can work for you. Scheduling is a must. A word of caution: don't fall into the trap of thinking that making your time work for you means you can multitask. When you try to devote your time to two things at once, you're just doing both things poorly. Set aside time for work and time for family. Create power hours, 1-2 hour blocks of time devoted to a task. To be successful as a Mompreneur, you must carve out time and control it. Constant juggling leads to burnout! Know you can't always avoid guilt. Carving out family time lets them know they are loved, and it's also good for your soul.

Guilt is crippling and devastating if you don't manage it. Whether you are just starting as a Mompreneur or you've been at it for years, you have to learn to control your guilt before it starts to control you. Every Mompreneur has struggled with guilt at some point. The first step to getting over guilt is knowing that it's perfectly normal, it's a part of the job description.

As women, our mind is always racing with all the things we need to do. As a Mompreneur that is amplified, it's now running a triathlon for your children, your business, and the business family that needs you. You have to permit yourself to not be a superwoman all day, every day, to all people. You can't do it all at once. No one can. Learn to forgive yourself for being human.

Easing your "mom guilt" is easier said than done. On top of being a mom and business owner I also homeschool my girls. They have lots of activities they do on a daily and weekly basis. To accomplish all this, you must switch your mindset. This is where power hours come into play. It's all about quality over quantity. Wouldn't you rather be the best mom you can be for six hours each day than a stressed out, stretched out mom for twelve hours a day? Wouldn't you rather be a focused, present business owner for six hours a day than an absentee boss trying to juggle conference calls and playdates at the same time? I break my day up into work hours and my girls hours. When you accept your limitations and find your ideal work-life balance, the guilt will start to melt away all on its own and you will accomplish more.

Build a strong support system.

As a Mompreneur, you are the go-to person for so many people. It's essential to have people in your life who are there for you, and don't judge you when you can't live up to your own ideal boss/mom standards. The reality is we don't all have a partner who supports our ambitions and goals. Some of us are single mothers or, like myself, have spouses that have medical limitations. You may not have family nearby, but you can still be a Mompreneur. Your children, at times, are your support system. Your friends are your support system. Your team is your support system. The people who believe in and enable you are your support system. You are who you surround yourself with. It is critical for your happiness, success, and overall self-acceptance to surround yourself with people who believe in and inspire you. If you don't feel you have positive people around you, find them! Look for your she-tribe. That is why She Rises Studios was founded and that is why we write these books. That is why we have built a community to support your journey.

Choose your team wisely

No Mompreneur can get it done without her team. When you have support it enables you to be the best mom and the best business owner. Your team should understand you and understand the empire you're trying to create. Make your mission and vision clear. Build your team wisely; it's critical to your success. Form a team that can take on tasks that aren't your strong suit and consume too much of your valuable and limited time. A Mompreneur's time is more limited than that of the average entrepreneur. So, you have to be twice as picky about your work family. Your team is your second family, so they have to support you just as much as your business will support them. Hire the kind of people who will not just reduce your workload but your stress load. Build a team that compliments you and creates residual and more consistent income.

Learn to master your work/life balance

As a Mompreneur, your family is the reason for everything you do. It's your core, your WHY. Everything else in your life revolves around that. Design your work schedule around your family and not the other way around. You're the boss, so your hours are what you want them to be. There will never be enough hours in the day to accomplish everything. Sometimes you will have to stay up late after the kids go to sleep to finish your work. I often spend 2 hours after they go to bed at night and 2 hours in the morning before they get up working on my business. The hours I spend sitting in the car at rehearsal, dance, and practices for my girls are uninterrupted additional power hours. I make phone calls, catch up on emails, attend zoom meetings from my car, or set my calendar. While I'm letting you in on secrets, here's an important one: working extra early or extra late hours is more than worth it when it enables you to be present in your child's life without guilt.

Hold yourself accountable

Being a Mompreneur is one the most incredible things in the world. It allows you the freedom to be present. It has allowed me to put life on pause to help my husband go through cancer, have my third daughter, and experience my life. I had no one to check in with, no time off request to submit, no one I am held accountable to. I can be present for the great times and the hard times. As a Mompreneur, in your moments of greatest need, you only need to answer to those that matter most. That's a privilege and a blessing you can never, ever take for granted. The second you do, it becomes inconsequential and you lose sight of why "Mompreneurship" is worth it in the first place. At the same time have a buddy or she-tribe to help you stay focused and not lose sight of your business goals during life's roller coaster. Make your tribe or team aware of your goals and ambitions. Have weekly or monthly check in days where you have someone you have to answer to about other goals. Accountability is key.

Don't be afraid. When I started this journey, I was terrified of disappointing myself and others if I failed. The biggest struggle towards my success was believing in myself. As a mom and an entrepreneur, you will fail or succeed on your terms. As a mom and an entrepreneur, we will fail or succeed on our own terms. I have found it's all in our mindset and planning. We don't plan to fail; we fail to plan. Find your mission; it will drive your ambition. When you have faith, combined with focus you will see growth. Again, remember that being an entrepreneur is a full-time job. Being a mother is a full-time job. Being a Mompreneur is an extreme sport, and not for the faint at heart, but it is the most rewarding thing in the world.

As women, we wear many hats. Juggling becomes our art form. The first thing you must understand and give yourself credit; being a Mom is a full-time job. Being an entrepreneur is a full-time job. Being a Mompreneur is a feat. Many people have never heard of a "Mompreneur" before. Even few have dared to become one themselves. We're a somewhat rare breed, but that's just part of what makes us spectacular. The dictionary definition is, a mother who is busy raising a business and a family. The reality is being a Mompreneur is so much more than that. As a Mompreneur, your clients, your team, employees (if you have any), and their families are your family too. You are responsible for providing for your children, and for your work family and their children. Mompreneurs are very aware of our ever-expanding family headcount, and it pushes us to be at the top of our game. Not just for ourselves, but for everyone who's counting on us. I have three girls. My oldest is in her 20's. I currently have a preteen and a very rambunctious toddler. I've been an entrepreneur for almost five years. In that time, I've aged probably 10 but I have also gained wisdom on what you need to be successful as a Mompreneur. Here are some tips and tricks for aspiring and currently conquering Mompreneurs out there.

Acknowledge your strength

I often hear people say "I don't know how you do it". As Women, we possess unbelievable inner strength. When you become a mother, that strength becomes otherworldly. Everything changes; your why changes. We are hyper-aware of how we interact with the world, and how it affects our children. Our understanding gives us strength, and that strength is superhuman. It's arguably what gives us our competitive advantage, even as we fight against disadvantages like; sleep deprivation, extreme multitasking, burnout, and rising above in a man's world. Own that inner strength and use it to your advantage, because it is your advantage.

Take time for yourself

As a Mompreneur, it's not just rare to have "me" time, it's a nonexistent concept. At any moment of the day, there will be someone who needs you either your children, spouse, family, clients, employees, friends. Like I said, we wear many hats! No one can function without blocking off some time for themselves. Self-care is crucial, even if just 15 mins in the morning before anyone gets up. Succeeding in all roles depends on it. Mompreneurs are always running up against the clock, so you have to be strategic with your time. Always be on the lookout for ways your time can work for you. Scheduling is a must. A word of caution: don't fall into the trap of thinking that making your time work for you means you can multitask. When you try to devote your time to two things at once, you're just doing both things poorly. Set aside time for work and time for family. Create power hours, 1-2 hour blocks of time devoted to a task. To be successful as a Mompreneur, you must carve out time and control it. Constant juggling leads to burnout! Know you can't always avoid guilt. Carving out family time lets them know they are loved, and it's also good for your soul.

Guilt is crippling and devastating if you don't manage it. Whether you are just starting as a Mompreneur or you've been at it for years, you have to learn to control your guilt before it starts to control you. Every Mompreneur has struggled with guilt at some point. The first step to getting over guilt is knowing that it's perfectly normal, it's a part of the job description.

As women, our mind is always racing with all the things we need to do. As a Mompreneur that is amplified, it's now running a triathlon for your children, your business, and the business family that needs you.

You have to permit yourself to not be a superwoman all day, every day, to all people. You can't do it all at once. No one can. Learn to forgive yourself for being human.

Easing your "mom guilt" is easier said than done. On top of being a mom and business owner I also homeschool my girls. They have lots of activities they do on a daily and weekly basis. To accomplish all this, you must switch your mindset. This is where power hours come into play. It's all about quality over quantity. Wouldn't you rather be the best mom you can be for six hours each day than a stressed out, stretched out mom for twelve hours a day? Wouldn't you rather be a focused, present business owner for six hours a day than an absentee boss trying to juggle conference calls and playdates at the same time? I break my day up into work hours and my girls hours. When you accept your limitations and find your ideal work-life balance, the guilt will start to melt away all on its own and you will accomplish more.

Build a strong support system.

As a Mompreneur, you are the go-to person for so many people. It's essential to have people in your life who are there for you, and don't judge you when you can't live up to your own ideal boss/mom standards. The reality is we don't all have a partner who supports our ambitions and goals. Some of us are single mothers or, like myself, have spouses that have medical limitations. You may not have family nearby, but you can still be a Mompreneur. Your children, at times, are your support system. Your friends are your support system. Your team is your support system. The people who believe in and enable you are your support system. You are who you surround yourself with. It is critical for your happiness, success, and overall self-acceptance to surround yourself with people who believe in and inspire you. If you don't feel you have positive people around you, find them! Look for your she-tribe. That is why She Rises Studios was founded and that is why we write these books. That is why we have built a community to support your journey.

Choose your team wisely

No Mompreneur can get it done without her team. When you have support it enables you to be the best mom and the best business owner. Your team should understand you and understand the empire you're trying to create. Make your mission and vision clear. Build your team wisely; it's critical to your success. Form a team that can take on tasks that aren't your strong suit and consume too much of your valuable and limited time. A Mompreneur's time is more limited than that of the average entrepreneur. So, you have to be twice as picky about your work family. Your team is your second family, so they have to support you just as much as your business will support them. Hire the kind of people who will not just reduce your workload but your stress load. Build a team that compliments you and creates residual and more consistent income.

Learn to master your work/life balance

As a Mompreneur, your family is the reason for everything you do. It's your core, your WHY. Everything else in your life revolves around that. Design your work schedule around your family and not the other way around. You're the boss, so your hours are what you want them to be. There will never be enough hours in the day to accomplish everything. Sometimes you will have to stay up late after the kids go to sleep to finish your work. I often spend 2 hours after they go to bed at night and 2 hours in the morning before they get up working on my business. The hours I spend sitting in the car at rehearsal, dance, and practices for my girls are uninterrupted additional power hours. I make phone calls, catch up on emails, attend zoom meetings from my car, or set my calendar. While I'm letting you in on secrets, here's an important one: working extra early or extra late hours is more than worth it when it enables you to be present in your child's life without guilt.

Hold yourself accountable

Being a Mompreneur is one the most incredible things in the world. It allows you the freedom to be present. It has allowed me to put life on pause to help my husband go through cancer, have my third daughter, and experience my life. I had no one to check in with, no time off request to submit, no one I am held accountable to. I can be present for the great times and the hard times. As a Mompreneur, in your moments of greatest need, you only need to answer to those that matter most. That's a privilege and a blessing you can never, ever take for granted. The second you do, it becomes inconsequential and you lose sight of why "Mompreneurship" is worth it in the first place. At the same time have a buddy or she-tribe to help you stay focused and not lose sight of your business goals during life's roller coaster. Make your tribe or team aware of your goals and ambitions. Have weekly or monthly check in days where you have someone you have to answer to about other goals. Accountability is key.

Don't be afraid. When I started this journey, I was terrified of disappointing myself and others if I failed. The biggest struggle towards my success was believing in myself. As a mom and an entrepreneur, you will fail or succeed on your terms. As a mom and an entrepreneur, we will fail or succeed on our own terms. I have found it's all in our mindset and planning. We don't plan to fail; we fail to plan. Find your mission; it will drive your ambition. When you have faith, combined with focus you will see growth. Again, remember that being an entrepreneur is a full-time job. Being a mother is a full-time job. Being a Mompreneur is an extreme sport, and not for the faint at heart, but it is the most rewarding thing in the world.

Olivia Radcliffe

Founder of The Bluebell Group and Creator of
The Mom Boss Society

https://www.linkedin.com/in/momboss-olivia-radcliffe/
www.instagram.com/thebluebellgroup
https://www.facebook.com/thebluebellgroup
https://thebluebellgroup.com

Boy Mom, Dog Mom, Marketing Coach, and Mom Boss Extraordinaire. Olivia Radcliffe is a much sought-after expert in all things marketing. Olivia specializes in helping mompreneurs scale their businesses to 6+ figures without sleazy sales tactics, so they can focus on what really matters most to them. She firmly believes that women don't have to choose between being a great mom/wife/partner and being a successful entrepreneur.

Olivia is also a Women Empowerment Speaker, Podcast Host, and International Bestselling Author. Her membership, The Mom Boss Society, has been featured as one of the top growing communities for moms in business. Spending time with family is incredibly important to Olivia, and when she's not collaborating with other amazing Mom Bosses, she can usually be found on a walk with her son and German Shepherd.

To learn more about Olivia and how she can help you grow your business, visit https://thebluebellgroup.com.

Baby Steps

by Olivia Radcliffe

"Freedom is the recognition that where you are now is EXACTLY where you are supposed to be." - Meera Lee Patel, My Friend Fear

My story behind starting my business isn't actually that unique, when it comes down to it.

I was discontent. There was a longing in my soul, a knowledge that there was a purpose for me, bigger and greater than the path I was on at the time. I felt this innate desire to stretch and to grow and to build something.

To help others. Make the world a better place. Leave a legacy.

Then there were also the more materialistic reasons: I wanted to make my own schedule, have financial freedom, and have the time to go to a yoga class in the middle of the afternoon if I felt so inclined.

If you ask any entrepreneur why they started their business, chances are some of their answers will sound remarkably like mine. (We entrepreneurs may be a unique breed, but we're cut from the same cloth.)

It is that longing, that desire, that inner knowledge that there is *more* that drives each of us to make that pivotal decision to go into business.

Far too often, though, I talk with women who have started their business only to discover that it's quite frankly *hard* to be an entrepreneur. They feel alone in their ventures, doubtful of their abilities, like they're a fraud, and frustrated that it seems like everyone else around them is making more and faster progress.

Does any of that sound familiar at all?

When I first started my business, I paid $1,200 for a course that all but promised that I would be able to quit my job within six months.

Nine months later, still very much in my job and not making the cool $50,000 per month I had put on my vision board, I started to feel a bit…put out. I did exactly what they said to do in the program! I posted on social media, used the right hashtags, wrote blogs weekly, hosted webinars… and still crickets. No, not even crickets. Just awkward silence with me sitting in the corner breathing in a slightly manic way.

Then those inevitable thoughts that plague every entrepreneur at one point or another (or multiple points) started to creep in. Maybe there was something wrong with *me*. Maybe I wasn't cut out to do this. Who was I to try to start a business, anyway?

This was my first lesson and unbeknownst to me at the time, my first uplevel.

Lesson 1: Success (or failure) does not happen overnight

It's easy to fall prey to ads that talk about how someone "gained 100 new clients overnight/went from broke to 6-figures in a month/insert your own unrealistic but extremely tempting fantasy here."

Who *wouldn't* want to accomplish such amazing things in such a short amount of time?

Before I continue, please don't get me wrong. I have seen some miraculous things happen in the lives of my clients, some true rags to riches stories. I'm not saying it's impossible to get 100 new clients overnight. In fact, I've done it.

But what you aren't seeing are the countless hours spent working towards that goal. The hundreds of decisions that led to hundreds of small steps that built up, one on top of the other, to get to that point of being able to gain 100 new clients overnight.

Success – or failure, for that matter – does not happen as a result of one big decision. It is a culmination of smaller decisions, smaller baby steps, each one moving you in the right direction down the path towards your goal.

I wasn't able to declare myself a millionaire and quit my day job within six months like the course had led me to believe. But I had taken the first steps. I had made the decision to start my business. I created my first website and I found my first clients.

My son took his first steps on February 11th. Like many parents, I celebrated the moment, cheering and praising him as if he had just run a marathon instead of taking three steps towards the window to look at a bird.

And you know what? He may run a marathon someday and, though I will be proud of him, I most likely won't remember the date. But I will always remember February 11th, because those first steps were the catalyst.

For most moms, being proud and supportive of your kids' baby steps in life (or those of your friends or loved ones) feels natural. What comes less naturally though, is learning to embrace your own baby steps.

We have a tendency to hold ourselves to impossibly high standards. We expect ourselves to be flawlessly perfect experts at something the first time we try it. We chase perfection, telling ourselves by doing so that we're not good enough as is. In turn, we reduce ourselves to one of two things: perfect or worthless.

Perfection is unattainable. And it is the enemy of love.

Which brings me to the second lesson:

Lesson 2: Self-judgment is the quickest way to defeat your own goals

Take a moment and think about who you love. Who are they to you? What are some of their character traits that you love? What are some of their character traits that you could, quite frankly, do without?

I'm blessed to have a lot of love in my life, but at the top of that list is the love I have for my toddler. There's so much I love about him, and I wouldn't change a single thing but he is so not perfect.

He drools — like, constantly. He gets grumpy if he falls asleep after noon and his greedy side comes out just a bit when french fries are involved. I love all of it.

I don't love him because he's perfect. I love him unconditionally, regardless of his flaws or faults. And I imagine that you're the same way. Those whom you love most likely aren't perfect. They have their own shortcomings and areas they can grow in. Nonetheless, you love them.

It shouldn't be that big of a stretch then for us to be able to love ourselves despite our imperfections. Real love isn't about honoring what's perfect, it's about embracing what's imperfect.

Younger me saw little bumps in the road as giant roadblocks and I would be unnecessarily hard on myself for deigning to encounter them. Now, I embrace hardships for what they are: opportunities to learn and to grow.

Leaning into challenges expands who we are and helps strengthen our relationship with ourselves. When we're put through tough situations, we learn what we're made of, because we are at our absolute strongest only when strong is the last option we have.

That means that instead of being critical of yourself for not being perfect or where you "should" be, look for ways to appreciate yourself, love yourself, honor yourself, and to value yourself as much and as often as you can.

Lesson 3: Progress comes from first being committed to the relationship you have with yourself

I have a history of abuse in my life, including verbal and emotional abuse. I thought I had escaped, but for years afterward, I continued to replay their hateful comments in my head, over and over again. They might as well have been standing above me still, shouting their words down over me.

I understood the concept of self-love and was desperately *trying* to love myself, honest to God, but I couldn't quite get there. It wasn't because my self-esteem was low, it was because I didn't respect myself.

Love doesn't exist in our self-esteem, it exists in our self-respect. Self-respect is the primary language of self-love. A lot of people make the mistake of thinking they'll earn respect when they "make it" and have success. Self-respect isn't about impressing others quickly. It's about impressing yourself slowly, by taking one baby step after another, learning and growing and developing a trusting relationship with yourself as you go. Self-respect doesn't come from being perfect, it comes from making progress.

So, in this moment, I want you to decide who you want to be, how you want to be, and where you want to be. Because if you don't decide this for yourself, everything that blows your way will bend you like a blade of grass and take you off onto another course.

Don't worry about jumping to the end goal. Savor the baby steps you will take to get there, and the exponential growth that will come with each one.

You are exactly where you are supposed to be in this moment, perfectly positioned to learn the lessons that will prepare you for the next level. Be committed to the relationship you have with yourself, because ultimately, to succeed you only need yourself and the next right step.

Angela Bell

The Inspired & Profitable Mompreneur Founder

https://www.linkedin.com/in/angela-bell-776a529/
https://www.instagram.com/i.am.angelabell/
https://www.facebook.com/angela.bell.3597/
angela-bell-8011.mykajabi.com
www.angelabell.ca

Angela is committed to helping moms create time & financial freedom through their own business. She is a multi-passionate entrepreneur, business & success coach for moms, and mom of twins. As the founder of the Inspired & Profitable Mompreneur, she uses her passion, training and experience to help other moms see themselves as the Queens they are and build their empire.

She has built a 7-figure food manufacturing business from the ground up, published 2 books one of which was an international best seller, and helped hundreds of women launch and grow their own Inspired & Profitable online businesses. Angela is committed to helping other moms live their very best lives, on their own terms!

In her spare time, you will find Angela playing with her kids and dogs, reading, baking, orgoing for a nice long-distance run.

Xo

Being a Mom is a Superpower in Business

by Angela Bell

Kids have a way of making the impossible possible. Having kids has a funny way of making it possible for you to do things you would never have thought you could. Kids give you mom superpowers. I know this from first-hand experience.

I am Angela Bell, mom of 6-year-old twins, wife, Mompreneur Business Coach, Best Selling Author, endurance runner, baker, lover of all things pink and sparkly, and fierce advocate for mothers' financial literacy and wealth. I have always been entrepreneurial, in that clichéd "paper route and lemonade stand as a kid" kind of way. But if I'm being honest, I was a reluctant entrepreneur. I was never quite sure if I was the entrepreneurial type.

I can tell you now, with absolute certainty, that I am 100% the type!

It took some struggling to come to that conclusion, that's for sure. I definitely doubted the idea when I was pregnant with my twins. But having those two beautiful humans only made me better at it. Some of the biggest challenges I have overcome on my entrepreneurial path, I overcame because I had kids.

My first real world venture into the world of entrepreneurship occurred when my family and I bought a little flavour company. I had just moved back to Canada after completing my law degree in the USA. My dad found this little company for sale, and we decided it would be a great adventure. Dad and I had always dreamed of owning our own company. Over five years, we grew the company from $200K in annual revenue to $2.5M. I ran the company day to day, and he was my mentor and most trusted advisor. I learned more in those 5 years of running a business than in my MBA and BBA put together.

In January 2017, my father suddenly died in a car accident. In an instant, my whole life turned upside down and got dark and heavy. I'm sure most people wouldn't have blamed me for throwing in the towel and giving up on the business. But things are different when you have children. Quitting isn't an option. You don't get to just lie down and let the sadness swallow you. They need you, the best version of you that you can muster. As a mom, you rise to the challenge, you do the impossible. At the time, my twins were 1.5 years old. They didn't understand what was happening; they just knew there were a lot of new faces around and everyone was sad. They were my reason during one of the darkest periods of my life. They were the reason I got up every day and participated in life. They were the reason I kept working on the business and myself. They were the reason I laughed, smiled, danced, and looked for joy. This wasn't the first time having kids had given me strength I didn't know I had, and it wouldn't be the last.

A year later, I had to call on my kid-given mom superpowers yet again.

In February of 2018, I went into the office on a Saturday to find the landlord changing the locks on the building. We were 45 days late on rent, and that was the end. For the second time in a year, time stood still as my heart broke into a million pieces. For the second time in a year, my children gave me strength I did not know I had. The business had been struggling since my dad passed away, and everything we had was invested in it. With the change of a lock, we had no business and therefore no jobs. Our assets were drained, our credit cards were maxed out, and we had bills to pay.

As I sat at the dining room table with my mom, rolling loonies and toonies to buy groceries, I vowed to myself that my children would not know we were struggling. They would not know I was struggling. My pain would not be theirs to shoulder.

So again, I found a way. I didn't do it alone, so many people helped along the way. My kids' nanny kept coming to work, even though I couldn't pay her. My husband worked hard to earn money to keep us going, and my mom and I got jobs at another food manufacturer to pay the bills. My kids had a great time using old gift cards and doing every free activity that we could.

I got through the business bankruptcy and still showed up as the best mom I could be, even if that wasn't great at times. I shouldered lawsuits, creditor negotiations, judgements, harassing calls, and even one of the lenders trying to take our house. I didn't let it make me bitter, because they deserved better. When I thought I couldn't go on, they gave me the strength to find a way.

Here is the best part: things did get better. A year later, I switched careers and became a mortgage agent. I got back into business for myself, because that is where I wanted to be. I didn't let one unfortunate ending stop me from trying again, in part because I wanted to model resilience for my kids. I wanted to be able to be present for them when they needed me. I wanted to create a bright future of my own design.

When the pandemic hit, it struck me just how much was being put on moms. Schools and daycares were closed. People were forced to work from home. In a lot of cases, homeschooling, online learning, and childcare are put on moms. Sadly, not all employers were understanding of the situation moms were put in. According to the Census Bureau, nearly 3.5 million moms with school-aged children lost employment, took leaves of absence, or quit the labor market entirely when the pandemic broke out in the spring of 2020.

It's funny how uncertainty and upheaval can make everything suddenly clear. It was in the early stages of the pandemic that my calling became crystal clear to me. When faced with the statistics and stories coming out about the effects the pandemic was having on working mothers, suddenly I knew everything I had been through, everything I had learned, had prepared me for this moment. I knew my purpose was to help other moms start and grow their own businesses so that they could have time and financial freedom. I knew I had to help as many moms as I could create lives that they had a say in and income that they could control. I became a Mompreneur Business Coach!

So many people will tell you that being a mom limits what you can do. They say it stops you from being able to be, do, and have all the things you once wanted. To me, that is absolutely FALSE.

I believe being a mom gives you superpowers. It gives you strength, grit, and drive. It gives you the most powerful motivator in the world— it gives you a WHY, a purpose, and a reason to keep going.

Being a mom is a superpower in business too. When we become mothers, we acquire all the skills and abilities associated with successful entrepreneurs. We can multi-task like nobody's business, we wear multiple hats, we can negotiate like the best of them (toddlers anyone?) and we can make magic out of scarce resources.

Having your own business makes life as a mom easier. It can be as flexible as you need it to be. You can work as much or as little as you want, or as your time allows, and your business grows as life changes. How much money you make is up to you. You don't have to call anyone if your child is home sick. It's freedom.

Here is what I draw from my experiences so far:

1. It will never go according to plan, and that's ok.

2. Failure is just a crap word that people are too scared to try and say about other people's brave, yet unsuccessful efforts. Remove the word "failure" from your vocabulary.

3. You will never be happy living someone else's life.

4. It is always worth trying.

5. It can always get better. Your life can get better, your finances can get better, the WORLD can get better! It takes work and you have to be brave enough to do it.

6. The things you thought would destroy you won't!

7. Other people's opinions say nothing about you and everything about them.

8. You are the only person coming to your rescue, so be your own damn hero!

9. Your kids need to see you rise, fall, and rise again. It shows them it's ok to get it wrong and that it's possible to try again, and again, and get it right eventually.

    Jump in, take the chance, and live your dreams!!

    XO Angela

Karen Van Buren

Warpaint and Ribbons Founder/CEO Karen Jean the Beauty Queen
Owner/Executive Director

https://www.linkedin.com/in/karen-van-buren-b21573111
https://www.instagram.com/karenjeanthebeautyqueen
https://www.facebook.com/1beauty1queen
https://www.facebook.com/livingoutloud4life
https://www.facebook.com/livingoutloud4life2

Karen Jean the Beauty Queen acquired this nickname at birth. Her parents would later see her flourish in a successful career within the beauty industry as an Esthetician and featured Makeup Artist for over 30 years. A freelance beauty editor, blogger, published award winning poet and international best-selling author her love for writing ignites her. She is a business owner, an advocate and an activist. Her work has impacted children to senior citizens from speaking on Capitol Hill to teaching in ministry to directing her own fitness programs. She has spear headed numerous women centered events, chaired multiple committees, been a keynote speaker, guest lecturer and peer counselor. A rape, domestic violence and cancer SURVIVOR who says her motto is to LIVE OUT LOUD! Family is her sweet spot so she wears her title of wife, mother and grandmother proud because she knows life is short and tomorrow isn't promised.

Bossy

by Karen Van Buren

To think back over the years of the many hats I've worn, I get a little exhausted. Most of my adult years have been filled with many roles and numerous titles. I honestly can say my favorite title has been answering to MOM. Playing out this role has been both challenging as well as rewarding. To be a MOM takes a lot of patience coupled with an immeasurable heart. Motherhood is fueled by the sweet, adorable, innocent looks they give us from day one. A picture stored in your MOM memory that never leaves, even into their adulthood. You're always reminded of their innocence as you grasp the process of learning them. This is why the expression "my baby" never leaves a MOM's lips when speaking of their child at any age. Being a MOM doesn't come with a handbook, nor do the hospitals send us home with an instructional manual. It's a bit overwhelming at first, but somehow through trial and error, we figure out how to be their MOM. Not one of us is perfect, but yet when our children are small they see us that way. They look to us to learn, for guidance, for consistency and structure. They look to us to be nurtured, hugged and loved. We are their security. We are their world.

The tables start to turn as preteens start to assert themselves. You become the MOM that doesn't know everything, but they do. Be reassured "this too shall pass," just like potty training. No worries because that "know it all" teen will either apologize, thank you, or both when they become an adult. Our kids see us as "BOSSY" while we're barking out instructions like a drill sergeant at times. That "BOSSY" stems from being overwhelmed most days. "Busy" is your middle name when you're a MOM. Often your needs come last. I'll never forget one time my oldest told me, when he was 7 or 8, that I acted like the whole world revolved around me. He was unhappy with my response to his last-minute request for a sleepover. I remember feeling offended at first, in disbelief that he wasn't aware that my whole world revolved around him. Everything and I mean everything! The job I chose, the schedule I worked, the numerous activities I volunteered for, to the friends I hung out with the majority of the time. Ultimately, I didn't take it personally because it came from his perception, and truthfully one's perception is one's reality. I understood my sacrifices weren't his burden to wear. I focused on giving him the gift of love, consistency and correction. He was expected to speak respectfully so being corrected for his disrespectful delivery left him upset in the moment. Oddly enough, it is through conflict that there is an opportunity for growth. Our relationship continues to evolve to this day. We consistently work on it by communicating. We strive to always have a bond that is unbreakable.

My sons are just shy of 10 years apart, but both navigated through action figures, Pokemon cards, Ninja Turtles, Power Rangers and video games. Both had their own unique personalities that I enjoyed immensely. Both were my little buddies when they were little. It's funny though how our children can act out when things don't go their way. Neither gave me much trouble when they were young, but that reminds me of an incident with the youngest. He was either 8 or 9 and we were walking out of our church. I corrected him. I believe it was for running in the church. He said, "All those kids think you're so nice. The kids you teach at the YMCA and here at church like you. Even all the kids at my school like you, but they don't have you as a BOSSY mean MOM." Again, I was offended at first as I felt with my oldest, but that was short-lived. I knew in my heart he didn't mean it but was being reactive to my correction. One of the best things we can teach our children is self-discipline. It helps them navigate our world so much better, without having an entitled expectation of life. Eventually, it aids in perfecting moral character while embracing harmony versus contradictory behavior. I am fortunate at this point of Motherhood to say I have hurdled most of the biggest mountains already since my youngest will graduate from high school in 2023. He's an honor student, he drives and has a job so my duties as MOM seem to have been minimized. We all know that being a MOM never ends and honestly, I look forward to the times I'm cooking or doting over any of my children. I am blessed to have bonus children also. Society would refer to them as stepchildren, but I call them my children. I'm proud to say I have 4 boys, 3 girls and 4 grandchildren.

Being a MOM is one role, but being a MOMPRENEUR has taken on many forms over the years. As anyone knows, the average entrepreneur fails at least once before succeeding. I have worked independently in the beauty industry on and off for over 30 years, but most times doing contractual work. I've also sold beauty products as an independent contractor and other products in multilevel marketing format. I have spearheaded programs in fitness and ran them for almost 20 years. Starting my own preschool fitness business was interrupted by cancer and a brain injury, due to the treatment I was given. That ultimately took me out of the workforce for a couple of years, until my healing started to begin. Using my entrepreneurial skills, I stayed involved with business while chairing committees and facilitating events. I utilized my gifts to contribute to pursuing my passions.

That is key: 1. Narrowing down your gifts. 2. Pursuing your passions.

I recently converted my "not for profit" liaison outreach to a nonprofit. I now operate my own 501©(3). I am the Founder and CEO of WARPAINT and RIBBONS, Inc. There is no greater joy than living out your purpose. We all have purpose! Find yours! Live it! Success is measured individually. Success is not synonymous with wealth. Offering yourself the means to be self-sufficient, while enjoying your work, is richness. The number one word holding any of us back is FEAR. It is fear that holds us hostage to invest in ourselves and push oneself beyond the limitations that held you back in the first place. You must be vulnerable to step out of your comfort zone. Be ready to grow because when you're growing you are never at a stand still. Embrace the UNSTOPPABLE mindset.

I thought that UNSTOPPABLE meant that "everything is perfect and you can accomplish it all" when it actually means that you are literally pushing yourself as everything is falling apart behind the scenes of your life. It means you force the resilience inside you to shine while simultaneously your mind is telling you that you are dying on the inside. It's when your heart breaks, but your spirit says you are not breakable. It's when you wake up, dread going into a job that is draining you, a boss that doesn't seem to appreciate you or a company that you feel doesn't value you. It's having a coworker working against you, who refuses to stand alongside you. It's being diagnosed with an illness that can limit you or your life expectancy, but you refuse to let it stop you. Or when your children go astray, and you feel like the world is crumbling around you. It's when a long-standing friendship ends due to a misunderstanding, but you push on. When your relationship is failing, but you know you can't fail yourself. Or, the times a family member hurts or betrays you and the decision to forgive is your only freeing option. It's when you face a system of injustice, and your spirit won't stop fighting for what is right. It's when your balance on your bank account does not reflect what you are worth. It's the nagging voice inside you that keeps telling you that you can and will make a difference. These are the times when you push and see yourself immersed from each fire unscathed and UNSTOPPABLE! It's when you receive news of a tragedy or death of a loved one and want to give up, but know that's not what they'd expect of you. It's when adversity hits, creating barriers that stifle you causing obstacles to begin the teaching moments. We find the tools we need, a reminder that we are UNSTOPPABLE!

Unstoppable to me is God reminding me to:

P.U.S.H. ~ Pray Until Something Happens!

This has helped me. And if you ask my kids what expression they remember most when I asserted my "BOSSY" (MOM) voice, they would answer "DEUTERONOMY 5:16" because it's me embracing being a MOM with God's help.

Last thoughts... It's okay to be BOSSY!

B.O.S.S.Y. ~Beautiful Optimistic Selfless Strong You!

To my MOMPRENEURS... enjoy the journey!

Priya Ali

Energi Living 365/President

www.linkedin.com/in/priya-ali-3237487
www.instagram.com/startliving365
www.facebook.com/priyaali
www.living365wellness.love
www.energi.love

Priya Ali, is a dedicated entrepreneur, wife, and mother of four children and four fur babies. She has led a successful personal and executive coaching practice, Energi Living 365, since 2007.

Alongside her daughter Aria, she also publishes an online magazine, Energi. The Energi brand currently retails a line of crystal infused healing water bottles, and is expanding their retail offerings. Priya also possesses unique intuitive abilities a natural born, third generation intuitive, psychic, healer and medium. She and her son Noah, also gifted with these abilities at birth, offer intuitive coaching, counselling, healings and readings.

Priya believes strongly that no two people are alike, and customizes her sessions and offerings to meet the individual needs of each person, couple, family or business. She has cultivated her natural talent through a wide range of professional certifications and accreditation to maximize her capacity to support the personal, professional, spiritual and physical goals of her clients.

Baked or Store Bought

by Priya Ali

I have been a Mompreneur since 1998, my four children are now 12, 15, 22 and 24. The age gap between my older and younger children, stem from a husband change. Going back to diapers and no sleep after 7 years was quite a shock to my system and I was further unprepared to begin the preschool journey all over again while raising my older children, as well as keeping my business going. When the younger children were born, I was still in the phase of seeing clients in my home office.

Once they both entered pre-school, there was some reprieve, but the trade-off was drop offs and pickups to three separate schools, with three separate start and finish times. Each day I had approximately four and a half hours from the time I returned home from drop offs, until I had to get back on the road for pick-ups. During that time, I had to juggle breakfast clean up, daily household chores, see clients, prep for dinner, and ensure that I would look like a Victoria's Secret model by the time my husband came home. The latter was often the one that I didn't get around to.

At this time of my life, I was holding myself to Wonder Woman standards which included volunteering at school, attending field trips, school plays and concerts, having well mannered, well dressed and well-rounded children, continuing my professional training and development, keeping a perfectly maintained home, healthy meals and an active social life. I began to struggle with balancing all the balls I kept throwing up in the air for myself to juggle. I used to be able to juggle with ease, like a pro, but I quickly noticed that the lay of the land being a preschool mom, had vastly changed since my first round. Playdate invitations were coming in printed on business cards, with a child's interests, family composition, email address and proposed dates on them. One extracurricular activity was not enough, most kids were enrolled in a minimum of three. Birthday parties were over the top, from the venue to the loot bags.

It seemed more and more was expected of me, yet nobody was adding more hours to the day. Slowly but consistently, every day I felt as though I was playing catch up, running late for everything, on to the next thing before the current one was finished. Each night I would lay in bed focused on all that I had failed to do, failed to do perfectly, or even a little better. Each morning I felt I started off in debt, for everything I did not accomplish the day before. Certain times of the year made it worse, especially around holidays and school breaks. The start of school, add on back-to-school shopping and resetting bed times from the summer. Thanksgiving, add on outdoor and indoor decor, super festive and delicious dinner, ensure all crafts made at school were displayed and ensure all children understand the meaning, and have something wonderful to share when asked what they are thankful for.

Halloween, add on great treats to give out, secure all desired costumes, co-ordinate trick-or-treating partners, outdoor and indoor decor, and attend all Halloween parades. There were similar lists for Valentine's Day, St. Patrick's Day, Easter, and the end of school year.

The big one though, the really big one, was Christmas. It starts the very first day of December with the advent calendars. I would then wait for the Toys 'r Us, Target and Walmart toy catalogues and nervously wait to see what was going to be circled for their wish lists. This particular Christmas, the lists seemed longer, with more sought after or already sold out items than any other year. All four children chose to participate in a Christmas concert with multiple performances, and multiple outfits and accessories required. Each of them had multiple teachers, requiring multiple teacher gifts to be purchased. Santa photos had to be arranged, as well as a time to decorate the house and tree together. The last week of school also happened to be one of my busiest times of year as an intuitive reader and life coach, as the end of year approaching, and time with family can create a lot of questions about the future, or a need for extra help with how to handle strained or tense family relationships, when tis the season to be jolly.

I was running ragged trying to get to every performance, to pick up and wrap every gift that needed to be gifted, and still keep up with the day to day needs of my household and business. By Wednesday, not only was I falling behind, but I was exhausted, and sleep deprived. I kept trying to soothe myself by reminding myself, I just had to make it to Friday. At least where the school stuff was concerned. Thursday, I had a client desperately requesting a session prior to the weekend when she would be heading to her parent's home for the holidays. I was supposed to go to the grocery store to pick up the ingredients to make a nut-free treat for Friday's party at Montessori. In my true, but flawed Wonder Woman mindset and voice, I assured myself that nothing was too much for me, and I would find a way to get it all done. In a moment with my higher self, I considered purchasing something store bought and readymade instead, this way I could ensure I had it covered. If only I would listen to the intuition that my clients paid me so well for, this story may have ended differently, but I went with the guidance of flawed Wonder Woman, "Pffft, store bought is not good enough, it needs to be homemade."

I saw my client, but things went a little longer than expected as she asked if I could do a balancing as well. This would take up the time I had rescheduled to get to the grocery store, but I couldn't let my client down. Suddenly, my flawed Wonder Woman voice said, "You can go to the grocery store tonight after the concert and get the ingredients then, you aren't going to bake until then anyway, and plus you still have no ideas as to what you will make." In the moment, this made perfect sense to me, so I stayed late with the client leaving myself just minutes to run out the door to begin pickups, get home to bathe and dress the kids and feed them dinner, before rushing out once again to the concert. The concert was lovely, and afterwards we were served lovely homemade refreshments made by the headmistress herself. We left and headed straight to the grocery store, only to be shocked to see it was closed!! I quickly began to google all other nearby stores, only to find they too were closed. I decided not to panic, I would just get us up earlier and pop by the grocery store before school and get something store bought. I went home, got the kids to bed and then berated myself for not having baked something homemade before passing out to sleep.

I woke up the next morning to the sound of the alarm, ready to check my daily debts when the horror struck. I was supposed to get up early, but I had forgotten to change the alarm. There would be no time to get to the grocery store before school, and any donut or pastry shop could not guarantee a nut free product. I was beside myself as I prepared the kids for school and began my drop offs. The younger ones were the last to be dropped off, and I pulled up in front of the school. The headmistress greeted the kids at the door with a handshake every day, so she saw us arrive. Suddenly I felt paralyzed by my perceived failure and began sobbing uncontrollably. The headmistress must have noticed this and came to the car. I reluctantly put the window down and she proceeded to ask me what was wrong, but I could not speak through my tears. She asked me if someone had died and for a split second I contemplated saying yes, but before I knew it I blurted out, "No, I have no dessert for the party". Her face crossed between disbelief and disturbed, and she directed me to let the children out to go inside. She came back and repeatedly reassured me that there were more than enough treats and that I had nothing to worry about. Easy for her to say, she made homemade cupcakes with fondant icing the night before, for the whole school.

Later when I picked up the kids and inquired about the party, they had a lovely time and were content with the snacks provided. Then they said, "now Mommy we get to be with you for the holidays every day". It really hit me, that all the pressure, the impossibly high standards and perfection were self imposed. I was not a failure in the eyes of my children, nor my clients, only in the eyes that stared back at me in the mirror. When I dropped the self-judgement, it allowed me to pick up true joy, the ability to be present in all areas of my life, to have balance, and to show up like a Victoria's Secret model for my husband a little more often. Be easy with yourselves Mompreneurs, and consider telling yourselves as I do, "Nobody has seen me and Wonder Woman in the same room now, have they?"

Erin Vandersluis

Erin VanderSluis Design
Interior Design Consultant | Entrepreneur | Model
www.linkedin.com/in/erin-vandersluis-4601421a0/
www.instagram.com/erinvsdesign
www.facebook.com/erinvsdesign
www.erinvsdesign.com

Erin VanderSluis is a dedicated designer, entrepreneur, model, mom and wife. Her business "Erin VanderSluis Design" offers interior and exterior design services to clients across the globe and her design work has been featured in OUR HOMES "Best of Ontario" magazine.

Along with her husband, Scott, she also owns and operates a reputable General Contracting business called "Bouma Builders Inc."

Erin has her Bachelor of Arts degree from The University of Western Ontario, a post-graduate in Public Relations from Niagara Collage and a diploma from the Interior Design Institute of Canada. Aside from design, Erin has a strong passion for outreach, dedicating her spare time to helping others in need and launching several fundraising campaigns for organizations in her community.

She's a true creative at heart and loves music, theology, fashion, and empowering women to find their passions.

Rise Up

by Erin Vandersluis

I got the phone call no parent wants. It was first thing in the morning on May 12, 2011. I was in the middle of a team meeting at my corporate job, not knowing the absolute scariest day of my life was on the horizon.

"Unknown caller," my phone read. "That's weird," I thought, as I quickly silenced the phone, embarrassed it interrupted the meeting.

Not even 5 mins later my phone rang again. This time it was my husband, Scott; rarely would he call me during work hours. "I better take this," I said as I excused myself out into the hallway.

"Erin, get to the hospital right away. It's Lauren," Scott said. Our 17-month-old baby girl fell in the pool at the babysitters. She was found unconscious and floating in the water. His voice was shaky. I've never heard that type of fear in his voice before.

Panicked, I ran back into the meeting, and without saying anything, I grabbed my purse and headed towards the elevator. Everything was a blur as I ran, 6-months pregnant, to my little Mazda 3 in the crowded parking lot and tried to calmly make it to the hospital safely.

When I arrived, a triage nurse took me into the trauma room. Scott sat, crying in a chair, as several doctors and nurses surrounded Lauren on the bed. She was in the middle of a seizure they couldn't stop.

I fell into Scott and cried, "Is she going to be okay? What's happening?!" No one answered my questions, and I'll never forget the silence I heard in return.

After an agonizing amount of time, they got her seizure to stop. The doctors prepared us for the worst. "If she makes it, she may have severe brain damage," the doctor said. "We'll need to do a CT." Our world stopped. We waited as they wheeled our little girl away to learn her fate.

After about 45 minutes the doctors came back into the trauma room. Her scans came back normal. We were cautiously optimistic as she was transported to an Intensive Care Unit at a bigger hospital nearby.

Over the next two days, by what the doctors call a medical miracle, we watched our precious baby girl make a full recovery. She was discharged and sent home.

As you can imagine, being grateful is an understatement. Stunned and thankful, we arrived home and soaked up all the moments we could together.

After a few days, something felt very heavy. I was due to go back to work, but the thought of separating from Lauren paralyzed me, especially since I had the option of staying home. After many conversations with Scott, we decided I would take my second maternity leave early and stay home with Lauren and our new baby on the way. He runs a General Contracting company called Bouma Builders Inc., so we decided I could also do the bookkeeping for the business from home.

So that's what I did. I decided to resign from my corporate job and be a stay-at-home mom and work from home for the next seven years. We went on to have yet another baby, giving us three girls in total.

I enjoyed it, I did. I felt blessed to stay home with my girls and watch them grow, but inside I felt lost. Once the girls were old enough to be in school, that feeling magnified. I felt like I didn't know who I was anymore, and I was without purpose.

Growing up, my parents worked outside of the home. I always thought I would too. I lived my whole life thinking I would grow up and start a career doing something creative. I loved the Arts. I went to school for Public Relations. I love music, philosophy, and outreach, but here I was, at home bookkeeping (it should be noted that math was my least favorite subject in school, and my marks reflected that. Ha!)

The next few years were a blur, and things started going downhill. I was robotically moving through life, passionless and slowly falling into a deep depression. If I'm being honest with you, there were some dark days. Really dark. I felt stuck and alone. I also felt a tremendous amount of guilt. From the outside looking in, it seemed like I had it all. A great husband, healthy and happy kids, a new home, a nice car.

The depression got so bad that I spent days in bed. I was completely checked out. It got to the point where something had to change. I was so lost, and I was at the lowest point of my entire life.

One day I woke up, and something shifted. Maybe it's called an epiphany or an awakening, or maybe it was because I couldn't stand to feel like that for a second longer. I got up, got dressed, and grabbed a paper and a pen. I wasn't going down like this; I was taking my life back.

I sat down on my couch and wrote down 5 things that I loved. Five things that Erin was passionate about. Not things that other people wanted or needed from me but instead things that made me who I am to my very core.

1. Helping Others

2. Interior Design

3. Playing the Piano

4. Philosophy/Theology

5. Acting/Modeling

I sat there with tears streaming down my face and stared at the list. Just the act of writing down what I loved felt powerful. Next, I decided that over the next couple of days, I was going to take one small step towards incorporating at least one of those things back into my life.

I started researching outreach programs, modeling agencies, and interior design courses. I remember feeling a fire inside and staying up late on a mission. Over the next week, I dusted off my resume and sent in dozens of applications.

Things quickly started happening for me. I got accepted into the Interior Design Institute of Canada program, finished my diploma, and launched my Interior Design business, all within six months. I was still working with Scott but simultaneously doing something creative I loved.

I joined as a volunteer for a local organization called Victim Services, which works alongside the police and provides immediate crisis response intervention to those affected by crime and sudden tragedies. We leaned on Victim Services when Lauren was in the hospital, and there I was, standing on the other side, able to help others through their own worst days. I started a fundraising campaign and accepted their Volunteer of the Year award.

I got signed with one of the top modeling agencies in Toronto, Ontario, and lived out my childhood dream of filming a commercial. I sat down at the piano and played again. I took my power back.

I look back and it brings me to tears. I decided to fight for who I was, and it paid off immensely. I had to dig deep and find who I was again. I had to rise up on my own.

Here's what I know:

What works for you is unique to you and our happiness is our own responsibility.

I know the battle we moms face between wanting to take care of ourselves and doing the best we can for our family. But I also know that losing yourself is never what's best for you or your family.

I know that no one, no matter how much they love you or want to help, can do the work for you. You have to do it for yourself.

I know that ruthlessly chasing your passions can be life-changing and that it might look different for us all. We can't look to anyone else to tell us who we are or what we need.

Lastly, if I have a piece of advice for you, it's this: please, please don't lose yourself. Don't ever forget what makes you, you. Don't give away more than you can afford to lose and if you are lost, fight. Find yourself. I promise you won't ever regret it.

Lauren Weiss

MCHC & MCLC Female Cycle Advocate

https://www.linkedin.com/in/lauren-e-weiss-female-cycle-advocate-00537a41

https://www.instagram.com/thescarletsanctuary

https://www.facebook.com/profile.php?id=100046109392085

www.cyclealign.com

www.cyclealignme.com

Lauren Weiss is the proud mother of her miracle child, Jocelyn. When Lauren's not spending time with her daughter, she helps women prosper in life, business, and health by leveraging the power of their monthly cycle with her exclusive Cycle Align Method™.

Lauren has a lifelong history of hormonal and menstrual cycle mayhem. She went on a quest to understand her body, cycle, and innate feminine genius. Along with her deep research and self-awareness, she began to feel energized, creative, and productive again. Her focus turned to understanding female hormones, cycle phases, and how women can leverage them. Lauren's research and a new understanding of a woman's cycle have guided her on a mission to debunk the shame and false understandings surrounding the female body and cycle. She wishes that every woman feels connected to their internal power and hormonal cycle by tapping into their own feminine genius.

My Best Asset

by Lauren Weiss

"Ms. Weiss, I am so sorry to confirm that you cannot conceive a child on your own. You will never be able to have a child, and if you do conceive, you will be unable to carry it to term." the doctor said in an apologetic yet clinical tone. I was in a fog, just waking up from anesthesia. "Did I hear him correctly," I thought to myself? "I must have misunderstood, surely?" I was 22 and recently married. My future was supposed to be bright and for the seizing.

I must admit that I was not completely caught off guard. I dealt with menstrual health mayhem since I was sixteen years old. I had been diagnosed with PCOS, Von Willebrand disease, and Endometriosis early on. This was my second surgery to remove endometrial tissue around my reproductive and gastrointestinal organs. The doctor had assured me this would not be my last. Unfortunately, he was correct.

I accepted what the doctor told me and adjusted my mind and heart to the fact that children were not in my future and set about having a career instead. Imagine my shock when two blue lines stared back at me from the pregnancy test that I clutched desperately in my hands half a decade later. I would love to tell you I was thrilled with this revelation. However, that was not the case. I spent the following three days in bed with tears and "what ifs" bouncing around in my head. The thought that kept coming up in my mind was "the business world views mothers as a liability, not an asset."

🏺 The Maternal Wall

Unfortunately, this is a rational fear. In 1971 the U.S. Supreme Court unanimously ruled in Phillips' favor in the case *Phillips vs. Martin Marietta Corp.* Phillips was suing Martin Marietta after she was blatantly being discriminated against and turned away by the receptionist for having a child in preschool. The receptionist claimed that having young children could affect a woman's ability to do her job effectively.

I wish this were an issue of the past. However, a 2018 study on the impact the maternal wall and other systemic biases have on women's advancement was conducted by the Minority Corporate Counsel Association (MCAA), and they found otherwise:

"The trends we found in systemic bias towards women and people of color were not surprising—but our findings for working mothers were downright startling:

- *Both White women and women of color reported that their commitment or competence was questioned after they had kids: 49% of women of color and 56% of White women felt that their colleagues' perceptions of them changed after having children.*

- *20% of women, evenly split between White women and women of color, reported that colleagues advised them to stay home or put their career on hold after having children—compared with only 5% of White men."*

How can motherhood be viewed as such a liability? Why are mothers encouraged to put their businesses, careers, and dreams on hold? Why does a woman's character, reputation, and credibility change after having children? I found answers and proved that being a mother is not a liability but an asset. I'll share why I found you should proudly display "Mother" in your bio and resume and how it ultimately helps your bottom line.

💰 Multitasking, Time Management, & Efficiency

I don't know about you, but my multitasking skills have become almost otherworldly since having a child. We, as mothers, have a lot on our plates. We're juggling multiple schedules and the needs of various family members and our own. Efficiency, prioritizing and pivoting become second nature. These are all vital attributes to have for a thriving business. Moms know there is a limited amount of time in a day and make the most of it. This allows us to structure our days and focus on the task. Being able to switch from one thing to another, seamlessly making sure we give our best to whatever is in that moment.

💰 Leadership Skills, Balance, & Humor

Being a mother means having a profound sense of humor. How else will we survive being peed, puked, and pooed on? This also means we know not to sweat the small stuff. Bringing life into the world allows us to have a perspective on what matters. Of course, being efficient becomes a given and is essential in business; we also know that if an email doesn't get sent out or we miss a deadline, it's not the end of the world. This flexibility and understanding make mothers great leaders. They are better at communicating, resolving conflicts, and being under pressure than most other demographic groups.

💰 Grit, Crisis Management, & Contingency Plans

Grit is a skill we learn through experience. It's the determination to do what needs to be done even when we don't feel like it. It's also one of the critical factors to decide if someone will be successful. The more grit someone has, the more likely they will succeed. How much grittier can someone be than a mom? Those 3 A.M. feedings aren't just a suggestion. Ensuring everyone is up on time, fed, and out the door to their respective places doesn't just "happen." Neither does running a business. I am the first to tell you there are days when I don't want to get to my desk and start on the tedious task at hand. Those days when you still show up when you don't want to will prove to be your success. Mothers are usually always prepared for a crisis or have multiple contingency plans. Do you know how many outfits, snacks, and plans we have packed away in our various bags? We must be prepared for anything. It's the same with business; we're often going into the unknown, and we need to be prepared to respond reasonably. Accepting change and letting go of perfection becomes a way of life.

💰 Easing Guilt & Ensuring Our Children's Futures

Being a Mompreneur helps us, but recent studies show it also helps our children, specifically those of us with daughters. The study by Harvard Business School Professor Kathleen McGinn found that the daughters of employed or entrepreneurial mothers often perform better in their future careers than the daughters of stay-at-home moms and are often just as happy in adulthood as their peers. It also said:

"Compared to women whose mothers stayed home full time, women raised by an employed mother are 1.21 times more likely to be employed; 1.29 times more likely to supervise others at work; and they spend 44 extra minutes at their jobs each week.

They also earn more money. Among the women who responded to the survey in the United States in 2012, employed daughters of *employed moms earned an average of $1,880 more per year than employed daughters of moms who stayed home full time."*

Often societal expectations put pressure on women to stay home and take care of their children full time. This is unnecessary unless you want to. The keyword here is what you want. There is no right or wrong choice, it's a personal one, and research shows children are not being harmed if mothers decide to pursue their passions. Let go of "mom guilt" and make your children proud. As we learned above, you have the skills to do so!

👛 My Best Asset

After the three days of turmoil I spent in bed, I realized that I was given a miracle. I had been told by more than one doctor that I would never be able to have children, and here I was pregnant! It made me wonder what else I could do—armed with this new mindset; I set out to prove that being a mother in the entrepreneurial and business space was not a liability but would become my best asset.

I remember the first time I held my daughter in my arms. It was love at first sight. The love a mother has for her child is like none other. It is pure, unconditional, and enduring. I can say that I am a better human being because of my daughter. Jocelyn has been my greatest gift and accomplishment. I want nothing more than to show her that she can do whatever she sets her mind to. That is why I became an unstoppable Mompreneur! I love helping Mompreneurs learn how to harness and use the power of their hormones and menstrual cycles in their business and life. Do you need extra support around your business? Or do you need a listening ear? Please do not hesitate to email me at bauw@cyclealign.com or follow me on IG @thescarletsanctuary today!

Pong Spencer

Owner of Makeup by Pong & Social Media Influencer

www.instagram.com/makeupbypong
www.facebook.com/makeupbypong
www.makeupbypong.com
www.facebook.com/makeupbypong

Pong is married to her high school sweetheart and have five children. She currently resides in Michigan where she runs her online social media makeup and skincare business. She also works with her husband as youth leaders in their church.

She has been in business for 4 years. Her passion thru her business has been empowering women and helping them gain confidence. Pong helps her clients by teaching them beauty skills and empowering them with her positive videos.

Pong's strengths in business are encouragement, consistency, dedication but also a balance between work and her duties as a wife and mom!

Her greatest desire for women is to know her worth in Christ and become their best versions on themselves. She believes we all have a purpose and when we know our purpose and seek to fulfill it, we can have the confidence God intended for us to have to be our best selves!

Discovering the Mompreneur in me

by Pong Spencer

Being a Mom is one of my most rewarding but toughest callings. I'm a momma of 5! So I have had my share of many late nights, dirty diapers, a messy home, sibling fights and bathroom hideouts to catch a little break! On top of trying to figure out how to keep my kids alive, my last thought was becoming a Mompreneur! I was introduced to a direct sales company and fell in love with their makeup. My youngest had just turned one, and I was still struggling to lose all my baby weight from his pregnancy, so makeup gave this momma that boost of confidence I was needing at the time. My friend suggested I start to sell it, she said I could earn free makeup and extra money. I always felt like a kid in the candy store when I got new makeup, so I loved that idea and I wanted to splurge on myself and get Starbucks. As a stay at home mom, mom guilt set in often when I spent money on things that weren't a necessity. I felt like this was my solution. Why not give it a try? I ordered my business kit to start my journey. When I started, I had no idea what I was doing. I was added to training groups and welcomed by so many wonderful Mompreneurs on their journey! The first goal they gave me was to have a launch party where I shared my business. It was supposed to be a home party. I had never done one before. I was terrified! So, I asked my mother in law to be my first host. Thankfully, she said YES! and there was no turning back from there.

Today I run an online business that produces seven figures in sales all via social media. I never would have dreamed it would be where it is today. I truly have God to thank for that! He opened doors and made ways for me that I could have never dreamt of. He deserves the glory for it all! But I'm not going to lie, getting here wasn't a bed of roses. There were many challenges and struggles that have arisen along that way down my journey in business.

One of my biggest struggles that plagued me was my mindset. Growing up, I didn't come from a successful family. We were taught to survive, not dream! My limiting beliefs and lack of confidence in myself caused me to hesitate to take action steps in my business. One of those was doing live videos on Facebook. I wanted to grow. But didn't want to do home parties and miss out on time with my babies. But I was not tech savvy. I was scared and believed no one would watch my videos because I had nothing to teach. But it was also hard to think about having to leave and do home parties while missing my kids. At that moment I had to choose which hard I wanted to tackle. I made the decision to grow my business solely online and take the steps necessary to become a tech savvy mom. The great thing about technology today is that there are a gazillion resources from Youtube, live trainings, Facebook groups or online courses. These are all resources that are very helpful.

I also didn't start with a clear vision for my business. It took me over a year to really nail down a clear business vision. This is something I wish I would have done right away, but during this time I lacked confidence and didn't view my business as a business but a hobby. My self-doubt would always kick in. I knew I could not keep thinking that way. I started to work on my personal development. Every morning after devotions, I would listen to podcasts on positive thinking or mindset change. I also started listening to sermons everyday about having faith and trusting God more. I had to trust that God had a plan, and I would keep walking in the path that He set before me. I have always been passionate about inspiring others! When I lead my team, my desire for them is to know their worth and see success in their own businesses. When I end my Facebook lives, I always remind ladies how loved and special they are and how they have a purpose! Empowerment is so contagious, because once I experienced it, I couldn't help but want to pass it along to someone else. Don't be afraid to connect with other ladies for encouragement! Facebook groups and hosting local ladies meet ups to share ideas is a great way to network and encourage other mompreneurs. Everyone is learning and growing at different rates; when you can brainstorm with others, they may help you with ideas for your business you never even thought about.

Last but not least, I needed to remind myself to keep my eye on the prize! What was my end goal? I struggled with setting goals. It was also easy to compare my success to someone else's in the same industry, but I had to remind myself that it's not fair to compare my journey in my chapter 10 to someone else's chapter 20! I had to stay true to myself! I had to keep focus on what mattered in my business which was my integrity! Every decision I made, I asked myself would this align with my integrity. I made a decision right away that I would never sell my integrity for a dollar! I have seen my integrity get me farther in business than my skill. I wanted to be a business person that my customers could trust. We live in a consumer society. But I want people to remember how I treated them and want to go the extra mile for my customers. I believe in working hard and mixing it with integrity, drive and passion.

Running a business is not for the faint of heart but I believe you can unleash the mompreneur inside of you by these simple truths and utilizing them for your business will help leverage your business to the next level and increase your sales tremendously! While there are so many resources, running a business online can be very competitive. The market may seem saturated and overpopulated but having a clear vision is vital. If you don't understand your business or can't explain it, no one else will be able to either. Don't make it too complicated. Others will have ideas on what your business should be but if you set out to have a clear vision, you won't be swayed by new flashy ideas. In turn you can focus on your vision and not someone else's. The most important thing for me on my journey, and I truly believe for any Mompreneur, is having confidence. Confidence is when you believe in yourself and your! When you start a business everyone will have an opinion from family, friends to peers. There will be naysayers, doubters and people who won't ever support you. It is crucial that you have confidence in your path and purpose in business. No one will believe in what you are doing if you are unsure. When you find something that you believe in and love, it won't be hard for your passion to shine through and others will see it! I also believe success in business isn't about what you accomplish but how you can inspire and impact others along the way. That's why it's so important to be part of a community. God designed us for community and even in business we can reap the benefits of it! Learn to connect with other like minded ladies in your niche or business. We don't have all the answers but we can learn and grow from one another!

April Emanuelson

Lifestyle, Exercise, Attitude, and Nutrition Coach and Functional Nutrition Coach

www.Instagram.com/aprilemanuelson/
www.Facebook.com/April.emanuelson
www.aprilemanuelson.com

April Emanuelson is a mom of 3, a certified LEAN (Lifestyle, Exercise, Attitude and Nutrition) Coach for children and adults and is certified in Functional Nutrition. She teaches simple tools that help the busiest of people to make lasting changes to better their health. Recently she has become a gut geek, and loves sharing the exciting new discoveries that are helping us understand the most important basis of our health, our digestion! Instead of throwing everything at your system hoping something will stick, she specializes in setting up a targeted plan based on your own unique system and life picture, for long lasting change! She also leads all inclusive, restorative women's retreats—where women can come be nourished and recenter.

From an Aspiring Young Entrepreneur to a Seasoned Mompreneur

by April Emanuelson

My first baby was born several years before my actual first-born child. It was a brick and mortar business that took off running. I poured my heart and soul into this dream, and it grew magically.

Initially, I imagined owning a charming little gift shop. However, I ended up with a 3,500 square foot art gallery and wine bar where the rent alone was $6,500! I had no business taking on a commitment like that at 23, but I was raised without limited thinking.

My business partner and I absolutely fell in love with an industrial space in the heart of downtown Raleigh. Industrial, yes, but it also had these wonderfully warm and cozy corners. Being right in the middle of the best nightlife area, the location was perfect for our new concept, an art gallery/wine bar. With a combination of local artists, savvy wine purveyors, and a lot of sweat equity from family and friends, our space became a living, breathing, collaborative entity. The featured art and raw talent were inspiring. We attracted the attention of the local news, theatre casts would often do wrap parties at our place, and Lady Byron, who played for Louis Armstrong, became one of our regular performers. Our place was buzzing and vibrant with activity and energy.

However, I found myself working 80 hours a week, taking naps in the office after the lunch crowd, before we picked up speed in the evening. At first, I enjoyed the pace. I was young, and the busyness also helped keep my mind off of any potential danger my husband might be in, as he was often overseas doing dangerous rescue work.

On one of his visits home, I miscalculated my cycle, and as a result, we found ourselves expecting our first child. While we were excited, I was also really worried. At the same time, my business partner was newly engaged, and her fiancé would be moving them to Australia.

How was this going to work, with both owners having big life changes ahead? I tried to imagine bringing the baby to work. It was plausible, but not ideal. As our son grew in my belly, reality began to set in, and the long hours became increasingly physically difficult. Desperate, I begged my best friend to move across the country to come manage the business. She was a huge help, but I knew deep down that I had to make a difficult decision. I realized I would need to sell my first "baby."

Ironically, and by no small miracle, I ended up selling to a regular patron on the day I delivered our son. It was like our baby postponed his arrival until I had signed the sale papers!

Flash forward. My son was one, and he was struggling. He was a colicky baby, had food allergies, and his skin was often dotted with eczema and hives. This was frustrating, but when he stopped making eye contact or meeting developmental milestones, I began to panic.

I was exhausted from trying to keep him healthy. I was getting frequent, debilitating headaches, and I was stress eating. The baby weight wasn't coming off, and my skin was a disaster. I knew our health needed to improve, but I had no idea where to start.

Then one day in the kitchen, I looked over at my son. He was sitting on the floor, beating his head against the wall … My heart sank. "Oh no, this is autism," I thought to myself. Fear gripped me. Worst-case scenarios ran through my brain. What would happen to him when I was old or gone? How would we manage this? What if he is never happy? I frantically searched the internet for solutions. If you have ever felt real fear for your child, you know where I was in that panic.

After much research, I found a specialist who had her MD, a Naturopathic doctorate, and a PhD in physical chemistry. I wanted a doctor that would look at his whole picture, and not just label him. I flew with my son to see her, and she did comprehensive testing. His heavy metals were high and he had pathogens attacking his body and immune system. He needed some intense gut healing. Ultimately, she taught me how to heal his body with food.

I feel so fortunate that we embarked on this protocol for him at such an early age. Through some comprehensive food detoxes and supplements, he began to make eye contact. He even asked for new foods! He went from not wanting to eat anything but the beige diet and having massive sensory issues, to actively engaging in and exploring new things! He was a delayed crawler, but essentially skipped it and went straight to walking on time, and he reached other milestones in leaps and bounds! Today, he is a bright, engaging 17-year-old who, perhaps, is a little too smart. I shudder to think what his health picture might have looked like if we hadn't discovered ways to heal his body naturally.

Unfortunately, his story is not uncommon. Today's children are the first generation of children to have a shorter life expectancy than their parents. This is so sad and is why I have become a mom on a mission!

So how does this all relate to my mission in life today? When I saw what food and natural medicine could do in my son's life, I became driven. I wanted to learn everything I could about nutrition. I lost 30 pounds and gained so much energy! This renewed energy also revived my creative side, and I even started taking up hobbies like making jewelry.

With our second child, I had almost none of the pregnancy issues, like preeclampsia, that I had with my son. After my daughter was born, I bounced right back to my pre-pregnancy weight. I was feeling great physically, but something was missing. I felt like I was living in the land of the little people, with no autonomy or identity beyond being a mom and wife. My entrepreneurial spirit was crying out for something. But what?

So, I turned that jewelry hobby into a business and opened an Etsy store. It wasn't wildly successful, and with kids, it was a hard juggling act. Eventually, I lost my enthusiasm. Not too long after that phase, I opened an eBay store. I had a fair amount of success, and while I wasn't fabricating, I again had little time freedom. We had also taken on investment properties, which were a lot to manage. We often spent our "holidays" fixing up a place to turn over to new renters. I felt like I was trapped in a loop of ADD entrepreneurialism.

One day, after a particularly tough winter of feeling trapped and lost, a hint of spring was in the air, so I went outside to sit in nature and try to tune into what my divine purpose really was.

I reflected on my journey and the most meaningful breakthroughs. I tried to identify what I was truly passionate about. What mattered most to me? And then my son's story came to mind. Sometimes our kids can be our reason or our distraction, but when they become part of our journey, something truly magical can happen.

To me, health has always had a fine line that could be crossed easily to unhealthy when stressed or out of balance. And throughout my life, I've watched so many people I care about suffer from various health issues. It's been sad to watch them suddenly develop symptoms that visits to the doctor don't really fix or heal. When we don't have our health, it's hard to thrive and be prosperous. Also, in our younger generation today, there are so many children with overwhelming brain loads. This is a relatively new phenomenon, and so few families I know have been fortunate enough to discover the answers like I did for my son. What if I could give others hope?

From this reflection, my true passion and soul purpose were born. I went back to school and learned even more about nutrition. I started a practice and thrived on helping people become healthy. Some gained new leases on life, but others couldn't seem to crawl out of the holes they felt stuck in. A common theme among my stuck patients was that they were typically busy women with a lot of family and/or work demands, many of whom also had kids that struggled, too. I'm a "leave no one behind" type of person, so I had to figure out how to help those women who were stuck get "unstuck".

A new aspect of my coaching evolved from wanting to serve these patients. Today, I am happy to say my Integrative Vibrant Life Program is changing lives in measurable, lasting, and holistic ways! Think of it as a concierge service for busy women who really need a whole team of support.

I love my team of professionals who are heart-centered, gifted women. They serve all aspects of a woman's life, including parenting, health, relationships, moving past trauma and triggers, business mentorship, guidance in setting healthy boundaries, and so much more! We love giving women real answers and watching them soar and find their own soul purpose through the healing they do within my program.

Jennifer Taylor

CEO of Sacred Connections Author | Coach | Speaker | Advocate | Mompreneur

www.instagram.com/jennifer_lin_taylor
www.facebook.com/jennifertaylor.com
www.jennifertaylor.blog
www.linktr.ee/thetaylorbrand

Jenn is the heart-centered CEO of Sacred Connections. She's been a holistic practitioner since 2006. She's a Certified BodyMind Coach, Reiki and Emotion Code Practitioner and Meditation Coach. Jenn teaches exceptional women how to catch their breath in life, and make empowered decisions using her exclusive BREATHE Method. ™

Jenn helps clients reveal what is keeping them stuck. When women work with Jenn in a customized 1:1 program, or in a powerful group program, they gain massive amounts of clarity. They finally gain momentum. They have more ease, more room to breathe and flow. Jenn's superpowers are her empathy and groundedness, and her clients feel seen, valued and inspired to boldly step into their authenticity.

Jenn's biggest desire is for every woman to realize she's a divine creation full of potential.

Jenn resides in Florida, is a wife, mom to four, and loves to spend time on the beach.

Slow Down Momma…Catch Your Breath

by Jennifer Taylor

As I look back, I'm shocked and surprised by how many twists and turns my life has taken, and I know you can surely relate. It's easy to feel disgruntled and disappointed if life hasn't taken you where you thought you'd land by now. I have certainly felt this way dozens of times. Over the past several years, I've been intentional about my healing journey, and I honestly believe the hardships I've experienced are the biggest blessings in my life. It's humbling, dazzling, and exciting to see how all these conflicts, uncertainties, fearful times, painful seasons, and gut-wrenching situations have shaped me into the woman I am now. I've come so far, and it hasn't always been an easy road to becoming an Unstoppable Mompreneur.

For years I was lonely, depressed, and insecure. As a child, I had a loving family. Yet I felt a sense of disconnection from myself and others. I didn't know my role, and I didn't have confidence or trust in myself. Therefore, I learned to rely on others to make me feel whole. Reliance failed me many times. First, I put my trust in my high school boyfriend. He was where I found my strength, and I felt safe with him. Sadly, he passed away from a drug overdose. I was devastated. My world was completely rocked, and I was only nineteen. I decided to run from the painful memories, and I joined the U.S. Army, where I met my first husband. It was apparent that we didn't belong together, but we were expecting a child. Again, I relied on someone other than myself, thinking he would fulfill me and make me feel whole. That marriage ended almost six years later, and I felt hopeless yet free from the emotional abuse I endured. My current husband, Dave, and I became friends fast and fell for each other quickly. I had never felt so seen and acknowledged before, and I knew I didn't want to rely on him the way I had relied on others. But it was hard not to follow old patterns.

Dave saw I was broken, battered, and worn down from years of emotional torment and self-loathing. I had believed the lies. I bought into the messages: "you're not smart enough" and "you're worthless." If you hear something hundreds of times, you believe it. I allowed my ex-husband to steal my confidence. It was time to rebuild myself, my life, my passions, and find my purpose. Dave was an integral part of my healing process. Instead of relying on him, I partnered with him on this journey of self-discovery. We married in 2006, and our marriage is stellar. Seriously. It's more beautiful than I could have ever imagined. Together we have four children. I was finally standing on my own two feet, grounded in my identity, and had unwavering support. Dave's perspective of what I was capable of, was far beyond what I could have imagined for myself. This was a catalyst for healing.

I was beginning to love myself. It was safe for me to dream. I tapped into a part of myself that I never knew existed. I was healing from old wounds, and I discovered my passion for empowering and supporting women. I knew my purpose was to hold space for women and their healing journeys.

After trying a couple different career paths, in 2006, God showed me that I was supposed to become a Massage Therapist. I officially stepped into Entrepreneurship in 2011. It was gorgeous, freeing, difficult, manic, hair-pulling, fun, horrible, and exciting all at once. I loved owning my own business and serving my clients. I hated the mom guilt, and despised being away from my family on nights and weekends (even though I set my hours). It took years to learn to set boundaries for myself and my business. I felt torn, and I wanted the best of both worlds. I wanted a successful business and a thriving family life, but I was too busy to even see clearly. I didn't even have time to catch my breath. I was simultaneously homeschooling, volunteering at church, advocating to end human trafficking, navigating my son's transgender journey, dealing with ex-spouses and lawyer bills, filing bankruptcy, foreclosing on our home, having health issues, and trying to keep my business afloat simultaneously. Does this sound familiar? Are you doing everything for everyone except yourself? Are you drowning in overwhelm?

Amidst this madness ensuing, I thoroughly enjoyed my career for fifteen years. My clients were gems. Such loyal, beautiful souls who I adore. Towards the end of my Massage career, I felt the nudge to go deeper and add Body Mind Coaching. I taught clients how to listen to their bodies, gain confidence, clarity, and calmness. It was magical. I knew in my heart that was the next step, so I listened to my body and retired from my thriving practice.

Next, I entered into radical change. We moved from Pennsylvania to Florida, and it happened quickly. It had always been a dream, and it happened. I relied on my teachings and tools to navigate it all. I began working virtually. It has been the most rewarding endeavor of my career, and I feel like I've got a handle on this whole Mompreneur gig, for the most part!

So how did I do it? I'll share a framework I created to help me navigate tough seasons as a Mompreneur. I pray it speaks to you, and you can begin to apply it too. It's called the BREATHE Method. My coaching clients are guided through this and it's given us all more breathing room in life.

Be with yourself. Embody, meditate, breathe, hang out with yourself, and see what shows up. Welcome thoughts and emotions as you're able. As busy Mompreneurs, we miss so much. Our bodies are desperately trying to speak to us. Our next step is within us, yet we search outside ourselves for the answers. We stay too consumed, too distracted, and too disconnected from OURSELVES.

Rituals. These are sacred ways to honor yourself and what your body needs. Routines can make us rigid and automatic and allow no room to ask what your body needs each day. Instead of creating strict routines or schedules (that you'll break anyway and become disappointed in yourself for breaking), allow for small blocks of time to work on must do tasks (like eating, grooming, etc.). Then also allow for flow. Get curious and see what your body might be craving.

Emotions must be navigated. As humans, we all experience the full spectrum of feelings and emotions. No shocker there! Our society does a fantastic job of making us feel less than if we experience "negative" emotions or anything other than bliss. How ridiculous. Emotions are physiological responses, and we have permission to feel and process all of them if we choose. Often our body decides it's easier to store them away for a later date. Sometimes that date never comes, and the emotions can turn into physical pain, discomfort and disease.

Access your confidence, maybe for the first time ever. Confidence is gained when you keep promises to yourself (most of the time...because you're human). Show up for yourself, especially in small ways. Learn to flex the muscle of celebrating your wins. It compiles.

Trust your intuition. Intuition is part of your design, and you may not recognize it when it speaks to you. Intuition is soft, quick, and easy to miss.

Honor boundaries. Oh the "B" word! You know you need them but aren't quite sure where to start. They are the bouncers for your time and energy. You need them, so you don't continue to say yes to every opportunity that comes within 1,000 feet of you.

Explore your values. Not your morals. They're different. Many women base decisions, relationships, and careers around values that aren't even their own. Here's an example. One of my clients told me she values strength. Yet as she shared this, her body wasn't mirroring importance or excitement. Instead, it was showing heaviness. As I coached her around this topic, she soon discovered that she did not want to be strong. She learned to be strong. She was raised by a single mom, who needed to be strong to survive. In her mind, strength was admirable, but her body was telling a different story. She wanted someone to take care of her, her needs, and her desires. She decided that strength was not at all something she valued.

There you have it, friends. Does it take some willingness and effort? Is it a process? Absolutely. Trust the process and most importantly, Momma, trust yourself.

I'd be honored to connect with you. Let's keep lifting one another. We are stronger together, and we cannot do this work alone. Maybe there's a tug in your heart to cultivate the life you want. Let's do it together; you'll see, you're truly unstoppable.

Reesy Neff

Omega Ecycles
CEO/Founder
Author of "Stripping Off the Labels"

Reesy lives in York, Pennsylvania with her husband, Brent as happy empty nesters. She has four adult stepchildren. She has one amazing granddaughter and can't wait for more. To her, being a Nana is the best job in the world.

While Reesy was born in Michigan, she was raised in Eastern North Caroline and considers herself very much a southern gal.

Her journey as a mom and entrepreneur is far from traditional. She worked as a Regional Manager for a very large bank for 15 years before starting her own electronic waste recycling company.

Reesy authored her first book in the fall of 2021. She enjoys spending time with her husband, reading, writing and line dancing. However, one of her most favorite things to do is to inspire other women to believe in themselves based on their authentic self and not what the world has told them to be.

How I got my step back in stepmom

by Reesy Neff

On May 11, 2008, I officially became a stepmom. That was the day I married my soulmate, Brent. Unofficially, it happened the minute I was introduced to his four children, ages 2 to 9. I know, right? What was I thinking?

My mom, my friends, and I have an opinion when you begin dating a man with four children. My best friend was super supportive. She saw how perfectly well-matched we were. My other close friend was a bit more concerned, shall we say, "concerned" with how a man with four children would "take care" of me. My mama, being the sage she was, advised, "Reesy, when you marry a man with four children, you marry the children as well."

I adored this man. I had finally found my soulmate after two failed and abusive marriages. I had my own money and didn't need to be "taken care of." I was well on my way to building a career in banking with aspirations of becoming a regional manager. I agreed with my mother. It was a package deal. All I needed was their love and acceptance.

Hence, operation Best Stepmom Ever began. I would go to work, come home, make dinner, do laundry, help with baths, keep the house clean, do a little something for my hubby (wink) and hopefully be in bed by midnight. This was my definition of being the best stepmom or wife possible. Where did I get this definition of a perfect stepmom? It would end up being my personal recipe for disaster.

It was quite apparent that Brent's ex was more interested in being a friend to the kids than a parent. She was the "friend." Brent was the disciplinarian. Brent and I agreed on most parenting things. We decided I would not discipline the children. What was my role?

I often considered starting a support group for people like me, a woman without biological children married to someone with children. I longed to talk with someone in a similar scenario. I couldn't be the only one with questions. I could talk to Brent about anything. This was the one thing I didn't feel he could completely understand. That's not a criticism. He didn't have to deal with non-biological children since I didn't have any. My ex was out of the picture.

Instead of starting that group, I kept working at being "perfect" while trying to figure out my role.

I figured it out quickly. I was not quite a friend. I was not quite a mom either. I did find myself doing a lot of the necessary, but not fun, things. I took care of the girls' first periods and any puberty issues, from bras to smelly feet, and the boys came to me with questions regarding sex. You get the picture. I took care of business. I was good at that.

Was taking care of business my role? It seemed to be all business and no fun. Being "perfect" and taking care of business left little room for taking care of myself. Their needs came before mine. At the time, I didn't think I needed anything.

I got the regional manager promotion at the bank. I was responsible for eighteen branches for one of the largest banks in the nation. I believed I could still keep up with everything at home even though I worked more hours with more responsibility.

Time does what it does, which is to pass. They became teenagers. Things really got tough. The first totaled car happened on Father's Day with the oldest. Three more would eventually follow.

As it goes, the bank I worked for was purchased. I got a six-month severance package. I was stressed. I needed a job. Finally, after six months, I was hired as a regional manager for a small community bank. I love my new job! It was rewarding, and I felt successful. I had the best boss and mentor ever. I had influence, and people responded to me.

The children were living a double life. Our house had rules and accountability. Their mom's house was the opposite. It was known as the "party house". The kids had a sworn pact of "if you tell Dad and Reesy on us, we will tell on you."

Dysfunction and chaos run amok. We had two kids going through rehab for opiate addiction, three totaled cars, a child in therapy, arrests, my brother passed away, and I began having health issues. The stress was wearing me down both physically and mentally.

In the middle of all this home life stress, my beloved bank was purchased. My perfect boss left. I went from having the best boss to having the worst boss. There went the only sense of control I felt. My once safe place at work no longer felt safe.

The new boss was so terrible to me. I found myself filing an HR claim against him. My tipping point came when he approached me about the HR claim. That wasn't supposed to happen. HR should have contacted me. I truly thought he was going to be fired for creating a hostile working environment. Yet, there he was in my office asking me to schedule "our" sit down with HR. That shouldn't have happened either. I called the HR department immediately. All I got was "we will talk with him". No firing.

The panic set in. I couldn't breathe. I was supposed to have my weekly meeting with him later that day, alone. I was terrified of this man. I could feel my heart beating in my chest. I raced to the bathroom, feeling the knot in my throat quickly rising. The tears started. I couldn't stay in the bathroom forever. I texted him from the bathroom, saying I was sick and had to go home. He was not complaining.

Driving home sobbing, hardly able to breathe, I did a search on my phone for "how to know if you are having a nervous breakdown". It's funny now, not then, the answer. If you are able to search for this, you do not have one. Screw you, Google. I'm having one.

I don't know how I got home, but I did. I was a mess. After the totaled cars, rehabs, arrests, my health issues, my brother's passing, and finally losing the one place I felt safe, I broke.

I had depression, panic attacks, and nightmares. I would wake up screaming. I didn't feel safe leaving the house without Brent. When will the next tragedy happen? Which kid will be in trouble next? Would someone else die? I needed professional help quickly.

I needed a therapist for the mental stuff and a psychiatrist for the medication. The medication numbed me enough to function. What was I going to do? How would I ever return to being me? My husband wondered if he would ever get his wife back. I wasn't sure. I didn't want to feel anything. Being numb was better than feeling like every fiber of your being is screaming.

I started therapy and began the journey of getting better. There were good and bad days; however, there was improvement. One bad day at therapy, my therapist assertively informed me I had to delete the kids' numbers from my phone and have zero contact with them if I was going to get better. If not, you will end up in a mental hospital. She was being very assertive. I was sure there was a van and a straight-jacket waiting for me if I didn't do as she said. If you are thinking that's not the way a therapist should do things, you are correct.

I left that appointment and pulled into a parking lot sobbing. At that moment, I knew I had to make a choice. That's what it was for me, a choice. I could stay in the land of numbness, or I could choose to live. I knew my definition of stepmom had to change. I knew my job had to change. I wanted me back.

I changed therapists. I worked really hard to find my way back. I was very determined to get off of all of the medications I was on. That was tough. I did it though. I slowly found my footing. My husband began to notice clarity returning. I was coming back and coming back stronger.

I began to redefine my definition of who I was as a stepmom. I had to set boundaries. I decided I didn't have to be perfect in order to be the perfect me.

I had to find a new job. My husband has been self-employed for the last ten years. He loved being an entrepreneur. As soon as he saw me coming back, he was determined to help me find my own business.

Step by step, I found my way back to a better me. I published my first book. I lost forty pounds, and I started my own company to recycle electronics. Most importantly, I have redefined my own version of stepmom. I say my own version because, here's the thing, the definition of stepmom can be many things depending on your circumstances. I love my stepchildren. In fact, I can't imagine loving them more if I had physically had them. Sometimes I have to love them from a distance. Sometimes I get to love them a little closer. I am a friend, a confidante, someone they can rely on, and as far as I am concerned, I am a mom.

I believe moms often think it's best to sacrifice themselves for their children. That sacrifice may not be good for anyone. That sacrifice may keep the children from learning their own life lessons. That sacrifice may leave your partner or spouse feeling like there is no room left for them. What does that sacrifice do for you? How can you give your children the best you if you are not taking steps to ensure the best you is available?

I have learned it's okay to not be perfect. In fact, it's often better for children to see you as human, as someone who makes mistakes. I say if you find yourself lost in the midst of the chaos, stop. Take a deep breath and figure out what you need to do to get your step back. Is it therapy, balance, help from your partner? Perhaps it's just a cleaning lady. What you must not forget about is what you need. Because if you do, you may get lost. Finding your way back from that loss is a very hard journey. Here's to hoping that if you have lost your step, you will find a way to get it back.

Nicole Sacco

Health Coach/Medical Professional/Breast Cancer Advocate/
Fitness Advocate

https://www.LinkedIn.com/NikkiSacco
https://Instagram.com/healthcoachnikkisac
https://www.Facebook.com/NikkiSac

Nikki Sacco is a health coach as well as a medical professional who specializes in orthopedic care, all while battling breast cancer and raising her two beautiful daughters with her wonderful hunk of a spouse. Since being diagnosed with breast cancer in September 2021, Nikki is determined to make sure that women incorporate the healthcare part of self-care into their lives, so they can live the healthiest and best version of themselves. After all, taking care of her own health is what saved her life. To be able to stand by other women and offer her support to help them reach their health goals, habit changes, and strengths that they desire is a beautiful and healing experience to be a part of. When Nikki is not working with clients and patients, you can find her hiking, biking, or running with her family.

You can check out her latest adventures on her social media! Nikki Sacco is a health coach as well as a medical professional who specializes in orthopedic care, all while battling breast cancer and raising her two beautiful daughters with her wonderful hunk of a spouse. Since being diagnosed with breast cancer in September 2021, Nikki is determined to make sure that women incorporate the healthcare part of self-care into their lives, so they can live the healthiest and best version of themselves. After all, taking care of her own health is what saved her life. To be able to stand by other women and offer her support to help them reach their health goals, habit changes, and strengths that they desire is a beautiful and healing experience to be a part of. When Nikki is not working with clients and patients, you can find her hiking, biking, or running with her family. You can check out her latest adventures on her social media!

It's True, you Can't Pour From An Empty Cup

by Nicole Sacco

Who am I and what is my story? I am Nikki Sacco, mom of two beautiful daughters (a teen and a tot!) I'm busy raising two girls from two different decades while working as a medical professional and trying to get my health coaching business off the ground. I am also one out of every eight women battling breast cancer.

I feel like I need to get my story out now while the battle is fresh, having just completed my chemotherapy one week ago. I am halfway through my fight and I am building more encouragement and spirit to save women and inform them in as many ways as I can. I was born and raised in West Haven, CT. A true westies blue devil who was lucky enough to be raised on the shoreline. I grew up loving the water, whether it was warm enough to swim in, boat in, or frozen enough to skate on. You can always find me walking around the city, following the boardwalk. I just always loved to walk down there and still find my way down there to walk when I get a chance. Being active is just the way I've always been, from sports, cheerleading, to dancing. Even in college and adulthood, I always find a way to stay active and try new activities like yoga, Zumba, step aerobics, and kickboxing.

In my early thirties, I walked into a martial arts studio interested in self-defense classes and I fell in love. I even found my way back to kickboxing and eventually became an instructor. As an instructor, there is a special feeling when helping people transform their lives and health. My oldest and I would have our mommy and daughter MMA days together, and it felt good to know I was helping her gain confidence to stand up for herself.

Three years into training, I started to feel complete exhaustion after a sparring session or kickboxing class. Sometimes it would take a few days before I could train again. I kept chalking it up to the fact that I was a busy mom of a nine-year-old, working full-time, teaching kickboxing and trying to maintain my own self-care routine.

In the midst of my sudden exhaustion, I woke up one night and found a deer tick on me. My spouse and I are always running and hiking the trails nearby, and I have been a bit. I woke up that next morning and there it was, the bull's eye mark, so off to the doctor's I went. This is where health coaching entered my life.

I was treated for Lyme disease. The headaches and body aches were excruciating, and I became obsessed with tick repellant and appropriate clothing to wear in the woods. A month after this treatment, however, I was still exhausted, bloated, and achy, and my attitude was changing. Blood tests determined that I had some deficiencies, and I was given some meds and sent on my way. But why was this all still happening to me? Long story short, I went to see a naturopathic doctor, and that's when I was diagnosed with Hashimoto's disease. It's an autoimmune disease that attacks my thyroid and causes inflammation in my body.

Everything changed after this. Everything from diet and exercise to my passion for helping not only myself, but others who are just so sick of feeling like garbage every day. What can I do and how can we feel better and more alive? That was a question I became so focused on. It was as if I was standing on the mat in front of my kickboxing class, wondering how I could reach everyone individually in my presence and as a group all together.

I enrolled in my certification as a health coach immediately and started working with clients while helping myself at the same time. I was getting back to feeling like me again. It was working.

I was on the mend. I was still tired, but I learned that I needed more calming ways to build my immune system, and that involved slowing down and incorporating more "me" time. As a mom, "me" time is tough when you first think about it. A lot of moms get stuck feeling selfish or as if they don't deserve this. I'm blessed to have a spouse that pushes and encourages me to take better care of myself.

I'm lucky that I have the mindset to charge ahead and want the changes and happiness that I deserve. I'm also fueled by the fact that I have two daughters looking up to me. So, setting that example for them to face your challenges and want the best for yourself is just so important for them to learn and see.

Had I not wanted to fill my cup, I would be so lost and nowhere as strong as I am now in my current battle. A battle that came out of nowhere, silently attacking me and growing stronger. This battle has turned my full warrior mode on and I'm determined to pass that warrior mode onto the Women that have been to the place where you feel "stuck" or get dealt a battle you weren't prepared for. That's what we do as coaches, after all. We're your personal cheerleaders, fellow warriors facing that battle head-on with you. It helps you to learn from experience and passion that wanting the best for others is as important as wanting it for yourself.

Most of us have been there, needing that push, a reason to fight, or just needing a change. We have one life to live, so why not give it a shot? That life you fantasize about or crave. I've pushed my coaching business to the back a few times already. I felt unfit, not ready, or too imperfect to push on.

Maybe that's why I was given this wake-up call from breast cancer. I DO have it in me to help others. This experience is happening for a reason. I could shrivel up under the covers and cry, or I could stand tall and figure out a way to get through this gracefully and show my girls that sometimes you have to fight harder than ever to wake up and go after your dreams, live your life to the fullest, and help pick people back up who can't do it alone.

I have to say that it seems so funny to me that self-care is what saved me. It's been the one step that I always took for granted and pushed aside for quite a bit there. Take my breast cancer journey, for example. I made an appointment for my mammogram as soon as possible, knowing that the pandemic had pushed appointments out pretty far. The day my appointment came up, there was flooding throughout the area, and I was worried about driving forty minutes to drop my little one off to be watched. I mentioned canceling the appointment to my mom and a friend, and they both told me to wait a bit to see if the water had cleared. The chances of me getting another mammogram appointment were going to be another six months away. Moms, let's face it; between work schedules, kid's schedules, and other appointments, why go through this when I had the appointment that day? and off I went. Then my course in life changed to the point that my life felt flipped upside down. I had to start putting myself first so I would be around to tell my story, raise my girls to be strong women themselves, and find every way possible to bring awareness to breast cancer and autoimmune diseases.

Moms, we always put everyone before us. It's almost as if it's an unwritten law of nature that everyone else must come first. We make sure everyone's needs and happiness are met. How are we supposed to fulfill that task if we are not happy and fulfilled ourselves? Think about it. Even in emergency situations, we are told to secure ourselves before helping our children.

It makes sense, right? If we have nothing left to give, how are we to help those who need our help?

So, what exactly does self-care look like? Sometimes self-care can be as simple as taking a few extra minutes before leaving the car to pick the kids up, or just going into the house. Those few minutes of just unwinding let you leave your day behind you and head into the evening hours more relaxed with the family. Getting up early to meditate, journal, or write down a list of actions will get you one step closer to your success for that day. Gratitude is another practice that I do every morning now. Just taking a few minutes to appreciate all I have and this life that I get to live gives your day a new meaning and purpose.

There's something about leaving your house wanting to be able to bring a spark back into someone's life versus just trying to make it through the day. Even though I have been sick, I still try to make as many people laugh throughout the day. I find myself going out of my way to be a little bit more understanding of others' battles that we don't see or know about. I smile more, laugh more, and I try to attend activities with my girls when I can, at a safe distance. My battle with breast cancer will not keep me feeling sick forever, but the drive and push to succeed as a health coach and a happy mom is stronger now than ever, and I intend to make this chapter in my life an extremely happy one after going through the bad part.

To all the moms out there trying to start their own business, keep your beautiful chins up and don't let those crowns slip. You've got this!

Kianna Martinez-Caver

Beautiful Features Boudoir
Boudoir Photographer

www.instagram.com/beautifulfeaturesboudoir
https://www.facebook.com/groups/beautifulfeaturesboudoir/
www.beautifulfeaturesboudoir.com
www.beautifulfeaturesboudoir.com/contact

Kianna is the Empowering Boudoir Photographer behind the lens of Beautiful Features Boudoir. Kianna is a passionate and talented artist who positively transforms the way women see and feel about themselves. Through overcoming her own history of body insecurities, she became inspired to further help other women do the same, so they too could feel empowered and see their worth.

Kianna helps clients learn to further love their bodies and find beauty in the unique features that make them who they are. Kianna's superpowers are in her empathy, and relatability to others that help her clients feel seen, beautiful and empowered to boldly embrace every part of themselves.

Kianna resides in Canada, British Columbia. She is a Wife to her high school sweetheart and a mom to two little girls. In her free time she can be found adventuring with her family or reading a good book. Kianna resides in Canada, British Columbia. She is a Wife to her high school sweetheart and a mom to two little girls. In her free time she can be found adventuring with her family or reading a good book.

How To Overcome Your Mom Guilt and Become the Best Version of Yourself in Motherhood and In Business

by Kianna Martinez-Caver

As mothers and entrepreneurs, we put a lot of pressure on ourselves to do it all and be the perfect parent and the booming business owner that we envision in our minds. Being a mom and entrepreneur is a constant balancing act, between giving 100% of yourself as a mother and 100% as a business owner. Some days, you will be the parent you envision, and on other days you will be more of the boss crushing your business goals. It's okay if sometimes you lean more towards one identity than the other. You don't have to be both,100% of the time to be a good and loving parent.

I always want to be the best mom to my children and the best artist/entrepreneur to my clients. The past four years as a mother/business owner have taught me that you need to put your own oxygen mask on first to be the best version of yourself for others. For me, taking care of myself is making time for my passions and purpose outside of motherhood. I am called to be a mother and an Empowering Boudoir Photographer. By making the time to focus on what brings me joy; empowering women to see their beauty in a new and positive light, fulfills a purpose greater than myself. We should not feel ashamed or guilty about pursuing the things that bring us fulfillment outside of motherhood, whether they are our careers or other ventures. I have learned that you can't pour into others from an empty cup, and choosing to focus on your career doesn't make you any less of a mom. It helps to make you a better one. A happy mom equals a happy home and happy children.

Becoming a mom and focusing on things that better me as a woman has helped me re-discover who I am as a person and overcome years of self-doubt and low self-esteem. Growing up, I had a hard time feeling confident in myself and my abilities. I had a learning disability which made me believe I was not smart enough. I developed curves early and thought I was "on the bigger side." My introversion made it much more challenging for me to make friends. I grew up with a lot of negative inner chatter from those around me along with increasing social anxiety. Despite these challenges, I was talented in bringing others out of their shell and showing their value. I made it my mission in school to help people feel included and good about themselves, even though I often had a hard time feeling good enough about myself in most aspects of my life. I tried to be the friend I felt like I needed.

As I got older, those feelings of self-doubt, insecurity, and doubting my value towards others intensified when I became a mom. I first became a mom, six days shy of my 22nd birthday. As moms know, those first years with a new baby are often both the happiest and most challenging years of a woman's life. Being only 21, the only friendships that I had were from highschool, and with a new baby on the way, one by one, those friends disappeared along with my sense of self. I realized I had based my identity on the people around me to feel accepted.

That first year of my daughter's life was very lonely and forced me to do a lot of introspection. I put a lot of my self-worth into the way I believed others saw me. I had convinced myself that I had lost my friends due to my weight gain after having my baby and fed myself the lie that no one would want to be friends with me. The social anxiety that I had developed in my past tripled and became crippling. Leaving my house made me fearful and was physically exhausting.

During this time my daughter was my light and inspiration to better myself. I knew I was getting in my way and stopping myself from having the friendships and experiences I deserved to have. I never wanted my daughter to look in the mirror and feel and think the way I did about my body. I would never say the words I said about myself to anyone so eventually, I said enough was enough. I was tired of feeling lonely, lost, and depressed. Tired of the energy that it took to be so mean to myself. I forced myself to take charge of my life and begin the inner work of loving and appreciating myself as a person inside and out. No one was going to do it for me, so I pushed myself to be the version that I hoped my daughter would be proud of. Four years later, I have learned that these growing pains were a necessary part of my life I needed to experience to become the woman, entrepreneur and mother I am today.

Once I began to get into a better headspace, I began to play around with Photography. Initially, it was a hobby I pursued that helped me further get out of my shell and gain confidence in myself and my abilities. It was almost therapeutic to this young stay at home mom who was just now finding herself in the world. My hobby very quickly turned into a passion when I realized how good it felt for me to have something that was just for me, that opened up a part of myself that I had been suppressing for so long. I learned that I was pretty good at it and that people liked my art. It gave me the confidence I needed to find myself after losing my identity; to take my passion seriously and become an entrepreneur (something I never imagined I was good enough or intelligent enough to become).

When I had my second daughter last spring, I began to think back about my past depression and body insecurities and how drastically my life changed when I started loving and taking better care of myself. I realized that I could help women do the same and help them begin to heal years of self-doubt and improve their confidence. When I photographed one of my very first Boudoir sessions with a close friend, I realized just how impactful Boudoir Photography was. My friend told me, after her session that when she looked in the mirror, she felt confident and appreciative of her body rather than self-critical for the first time in her life.

After hearing her tell me how much this helped her heal past trauma and elevate her confidence, I knew I had found my purpose. I had managed to change the way another woman saw herself and inspired her to work on loving her body, so her son would grow up loving his. It was incredible.

I am a firm believer that we each have a purpose. I am a mom, but being a mom is a part of my identity, not my entire character. I am called to be the mother of two sweet little girls that have my whole heart; I am also called to be an empowering Boudoir Photographer that transforms the way women see and feel about themselves. Finding the time for myself to focus on something that fulfills me creatively has given me back my identity outside of being a mom. I've learned over time that it isn't selfish to want to have an identity outside of motherhood. It's okay to want to be more and find purpose and fulfillment in other avenues of your life that bring you joy. Not just for you, but also your family. Yes, it is okay to have more than one purpose, Yes you can be more, and Yes, you are more.

Ashley Pakulski

The Mompreneur Coach

Mindset | Productivity | Time Management

http://linkedin.com/in/ashley-pakulski-450417154

www.Instagram.com/ashleypakulski

www.Facebook.com/groups/themompreneurcoach/

Ashley Pakulski born and raised in Canada still residing there with her two most precious loves! Her daughter and her pup. She is a single mom and she is also a Mompreneur Coach! Ashley helps mompreneurs take back their time! During the beginning of the pandemic, she decided to go all in and launch her business. Ashley has a Community and Justice Diploma. She has hosted and spoken at several events. It has always been a passion of hers to help transform people's lives. Her expertise is in Mindset, Productivity, and Time Management. Ashley truly believes when you do the inner work you get to see what is getting in your own way and that helps you start becoming in the driver seat of your life.

Ashley Pakulski born and raised in Canada still residing there with her two most precious loves! Her daughter and her pup. She is a single mom and she is also a Mompreneur Coach! Ashley helps mompreneurs take back their time! During the beginning of the pandemic, she decided to go all in and launch her business. Ashley has a Community and Justice Diploma. She has hosted and spoken at several events. It has always been a passion of hers to help transform people's lives. Her expertise is in Mindset, Productivity, and Time Management. Ashley truly believes when you do the inner work you get to see what is getting in your own way and that helps you start becoming in the driver seat of your life.

Getting Out of Your Own Way & Focusing on What Matters Most YOU!

by Ashley Pakulski

Since a young age, I have experienced trauma in my life. I have a great family, but like any family or person, everyone has a story. Everyone has their own challenges and their own unique stories of who they are, which later in life impact their daily results and habits!

I felt like I was fighting myself, but in reality, now that I understood my inner child, I was discovering who I was! I had so much anger and hurt, and I felt alone. I felt that I was unloved, had no belief in myself, no confidence, and was searching for love in the wrong places. Aside from God, my family, and pizza, the only person I should have loved so much was MYSELF! Like a good friend told me, "You need to love yourself first!"

My friends always joked that I was always the type of person who always thought that the grass was greener on the other side. At one point in my life, I experimented with drugs and turned to alcohol. The alcohol lingered for many years, off and on. Mind you, I do have so many good and wonderful experiences, and just like a good friend of mine joked, "Hey, we experienced it all and are very lucky, just like cats who have had 9 lives!" My life wasn't perfect, but one thing I can say is that I do not regret my story. My journey and my story have developed me to become the woman I am today. This is why I love and help moms transform their lives. I have no shame or guilt. I embrace it all! As moms, we can have a hard time, even with mom guilt, having that time, and freedom. We all have past stories, limiting beliefs, trauma, etc. that are actually playing a huge role in keeping you stuck and affecting your productivity and results throughout the day! which I will get into more and give you something that will help transform your life.

It didn't begin all that quickly! I had my daughter at a nice young age. When she was born, I remember holding her and saying I need to do something with my life to be the best mother I can be and give her the best life. I went to college, I had jobs, I was doing it all, but I was still UNHAPPY! I felt trapped in the relationship I was in, and when it fell apart, I felt for a long time like I had failed my daughter and myself. I had a limiting belief that I later uncovered that everything I touched broke! That was the one thing that was keeping me stuck in so many areas of my life. I had my battles and heck, no one is perfect, but I am so beyond grateful that when I was beginning my journey (without realizing I was on my journey), I was a very good mom. I raised my little girl to know her worth. I raised her so well that she knows how to deal with and work through her emotions. I raised her so well that she knows what is important for her and what to focus on. Most of all, she believes and sees that the grass is always greener on the other side. I DID THAT, no one else! I remember going through my journey of finding myself and healing, but it's like I was coaching her along the way about life and raising this little resilient queen!

For many years, I felt that I was holding down so many things emotionally and even things that were weighing me down trying to manage them all. I'm sure you can relate. My story and your story can be different, but there is a reason and it is relatable to things. Keeping my head above the water was one, and I'm sure there are times you feel the same too. All I was trying to do was be a good mom, raise my daughter, and figure out what in the world was meant for me here.

I thank God every single day for my break free and breakthrough moments, including the relationship between myself and my daughter's father ending. I count my blessings for everything because this gives me a chance to be the woman I am becoming. A new beginning and the most amazing thing of it all is that my daughter and I are a TEAM! We are doing this all TOGETHER! I came to realize I can't control people, and one thing I can do is raise my daughter to have tools to support her growth within herself. People will make excuses, but she knows her worth and she knows what she accepts and doesn't. Most importantly, she doesn't stoop to the level of holding any resentment and she always forgives. WHY? It's because I raised her that way! See, you can know people's actions but you don't have to always react. When you start to work on yourself and your growth, you learn what is worth it and what isn't. Your journey of working on yourself and your business is exactly what's going to guide you to raising your resilient and amazing children! Time is a valuable asset. So is your energy. These are things that can hold you back, but you picture yourself right now being the bird that is breaking free, spreading her wings, and flying away!

I want to share with you some tools that have helped me along my journey. When I started my business, it wasn't easy. Heck, I didn't know what I was doing! There is my favorite saying by Marie Forleo, "Everything is Figureoutable!" and by Bob Marley, "Every little thing is going to be alright!" I had people close to me tell me what kind of coach I should be and told me don't start a business because it's hard. I had my family tell me I would always have NOTHING! Who am I? I had the people closest to me laugh at me and MY DREAMS. Hilarious right?! Guess what? That is due to their own insecurities and fears, which they are projecting onto YOU! I cared too much about what people used to think of me! Now I am unfiltered! How I run my business, how I show up, and being my UNIQUE self is what makes me HAPPY! I LOVE ME! It hasn't always been easy, but one thing I say is that we all have things that get in our way and keep us stuck. This is stuff that stems from childhood.

These are emotions, thoughts, and/or people weighing you down. See, my friend, it's not always about the time management hacks and apps that are going to save you! Do you notice that you make your to-do list and set your goals, but nothing or little gets done? Well, I want to assure you that nothing is going to change because this all stems from your thoughts, which cause your feelings, which cause your actions and results.

I want to share with you some things that pop up when you're starting your journey as a mompreneur! You are going to have many fears and excuses that are going to pop up. Let me tell you something, mama: the time will never be right! You have to work on yourself to fuel yourself up and grow. Everything is up to you and not anybody else. You need to be putting yourself first!

I know that things may be busy for you and, heck, you don't have enough time for yourself. So, I want to share the simplest tip you can start implementing EVERY SINGLE DAY! That is YOUR personal time and space for self-improvement!

This is called creating a MORNING AND NIGHT ROUTINE! Actually, I started implementing an AFTERNOON check in ROUTINE. I did this at the beginning of my journey and it has transformed my days and my inner self! My friend, working on a business isn't just THAT! You are working on yourself too! You are investing in your inner work and growth so you can become the woman you need to be in order to achieve that goal you desire! It's working through all the things that are holding you back and getting in your way so you can set yourself FREE!

Mama, everything is on repeat. I want you to observe yourself day to day from months ago to a year ago! Yes, things change and you have grown SO MUCH, but if you aren't getting the results you want, it's time to get clear as to why! I'm telling you it's not just about selling, or how you speak to your clients (which yes, it is), BUT it's all about how you believe in yourself and the world. It is your subconscious mind that's playing out your actions and making them a reality. It's your habits!

Things you can include in your routines:

Working out

Prayers

Lemon water, supplements, healthy meals

Exercise and/or stretching

Walking in nature

Gratitude/journaling

Breathwork/meditation

Affirmations

Personal Development/Podcast/Books/Videos

Working on being that person you need to be, as if she's already that woman who has her goal, she envisions Reading a chapter a day of a self-help or motivational book

If you focus on this on a daily basis, you will notice that the one hour you set aside for yourself will benefit not only you, but also your business, family, and relationships. I want to leave another valuable piece of information for you: If you are in an energy state where you are constantly stressed and in chaos, NOTHING is going to work out because you are FORCING it! You need to be in a place of alignment, love, kindness, belief, and action-getter to get the results you want. Fear and belief do not go together! This is why I stand strong and believe you do not need to WORK HARD to get what you want! That is damaging! You need to work smarter, to work less! And you must FIRST TAKE CARE OF YOURSELF! Take this all in with love and start incorporating it! This is the beginning of the foundation but will ALWAYS be part of your journey and growth. If you don't start this now, one way it will resurface in emotions, thoughts, challenges, and stressors is that you will eventually have to work through it! When you work on yourself and use these tools, know that life always happens and when you do, these things can pop up, but you will be in alignment and handle things differently, including your time management, because of these tools!

You will be in the driver's seat of your life!

I want to leave you with this affirmation today: I'm dedicated to self-improvement so I can be my best self and achieve my desired results. I release all the things that don't serve me and I am open to receiving all the abundance coming my way!

With Love,

Ashley

Gina Redzanic

Certified Business Coach
Network Marketing Millionaire
Industry Top Leader
Published Author

https://www.linkedin.com/in/♂gina-redzanic♀-2129b0160/
https://www.instagram.com/gina_redzanic/
https://www.facebook.com/gina.pantanoredzanic
www.ginaredzanic.com

Gina Redzanic is a self-made network marketing millionaire, Success Coach, and Maxwell Certified Speaker and Trainer specializing in Leadership Development. She is happily married and as a busy mom of 2 daughters, Gina balances motherhood and her career through many of the habits and practices she teaches her clients and team. Gina has been featured in Yahoo! Finance, named as one of the Top 10 Leadership Coaches in Influencive, is an Executive Contributor for Brainz Magazine and is a contributing author in the best-selling network marketing book series, Momentum Makers. Her speaking and training is often centered around helping women feel empowered as her passion is to build confidence in others. Gina is God-driven and Goal-driven and she uses personal development techniques to help others break down their business blocks, build belief, take control of their future, and reach success without the presence of "burnout."

Belief Drives Behavior

by Gina Redzanic

Close your eyes and take a few deep breaths. Imagine you are the future YOU, the woman who just went for it, and now you have achieved your goals. What does that feel like? What does it look like? What are you wearing? What are you celebrating? Who is with you? Look at all the details. Seriously, I want you to truly imagine this life you have created. Now close your eyes and visualize this for a few moments.

Ok, welcome back! How did that feel to get lost in living as "the future YOU?" That feeling attached with your thoughts is powerful my friends. You see, you can't manifest an outcome by simply thinking about what you want, you have to attach your emotion to the thought.

Let's dive even deeper. It is more than just thinking about what you want and feeling great about it... You have to believe it for yourself. Let me ask you to rate your belief of reaching that vision you just had moments ago when I asked you to close your eyes. Do you BELIEVE you will achieve it? BELIEF. The hard truth is that belief drives behavior. Behavior is what you do, it is the action you take, it is the goals you set and then make happen. On the flip side, behavior can also be a lack of action. Your behavior can be that you "get ready to get ready" and never really take the necessary action to move forward. So, what can cause you to freeze up and get stuck in avoidance? Lack of belief! This is where we have to start and why I am focusing on this topic for you!

Napoleon Hill is a master, and he says two things can kill your dreams.

1. Lack of faith

2. Lack of confidence

So many women yearn for the life they imagine for themselves. Perhaps it is starting their own small business or a leadership role in a company, or saying YES to new opportunities, yet they don't have faith they can do it, and/or they lack the confidence in themselves. Having a strong faith and strong confidence will build your belief. Once your belief is there you will be bulletproof and unstoppable.

How do you start? Let's first peel back the layers. You need to recognize some fears you may have that can be holding you back. Check all that apply for you.

1. **Fear of failure**: fear of failure (also called "atychiphobia") is when we allow that fear to stop us doing the things that can move us forward to achieve our goals. We are so afraid to fail, that we won't even try. However, every successful woman has endured many failures, they just choose to learn from them and continue on.

2. **Fear of success**: The fear of success involves being afraid of achievement, often to the point that people will sabotage themselves. While success is generally viewed as desirable, there are reasons why people may be fearful of doing too well. It is important to recognize that people often don't fear success itself and this can be caused from deeper reasons stemming from childhood.

3. **Fear of judgement**: This fear, in most cases, is a reflection of our own insecurities. So when you fear someone is judging you, what you're really doing is judging yourself AND the other person.

a. You assume you've done something that is going to cause a negative judgement. This is a reflection of your own fears.

b. You assume the other person feels the same way about that action and will also judge you. This is a projection of your own thoughts onto someone else.

Of course, these two assumptions are often incorrect.

4. **Fear of rejection**: The fear of rejection is being afraid of unacceptance by the people around you. It could be you are scared of people not accepting your appearance, behaviors, the way you speak, or your decisions. Or it could mean you avoid moving forward in your career and business because you don't want to risk hearing "no" which of course is just part of business.

5. **Fear of overwhelm**: Emotional overwhelm is a state of being disturbed by intense emotion that is difficult to manage. It can affect your ability to think and act rationally. It could also prevent you from performing daily tasks. Some women feel paralyzed to move forward in accomplishing big goals because they want to avoid overwhelm. The truth is, you need to manage your time and tasks, and move forward so you don't sabotage success by paralysis.

Write down all the above "fears" that affect you. Self-Awareness is the first step! Next, journal about how these fears may be negatively impacting your belief in self.

Another reference to Napoleon Hill is his suggestion to make "building confidence" and "focusing on your thoughts connected to emotion" a daily habit. You should spend 10 minutes every day on confidence building practices. You also should spend 30 minutes every day focusing on your vision for your future. These daily habits will build belief, and belief drives behavior, and your behavior is your actions... and you guessed it the ACTION will lead to results. Many women go about grinding and take action without the precursor of building confidence, faith, belief and behavior. When this happens, the action has no real energy behind it. It often will appear you are busy and hustling but there is no real result. On the contrary if you are avoiding action because you stay stuck in your "building self" mode, you also will not reach that desired result. So, it MUST be a chain reaction.

A little back story about me... I truly believe I have created my life and results by design. I did this through daily practices which in turn became habits. In 2009 my husband and I both lost our jobs; at the time we were about to have our first child. We decided to start our own business and the entrepreneur in me was born. We created and built a fitness business, one of the first boot camp style workouts, this is before the Orange Theory and other group fitness businesses even emerged. After having my 2nd daughter and while running the fitness business, I also partnered with a network marketing company and built that into a 7-figure business, and still growing and mentoring leaders today. In 2020, I joined the Maxwell Leadership program and became a Certified Business Coach and Speaker. I am proud of all the accomplishments and what I have been able to create but what is most important to note is that since my job layoff in 2009, my journey has been one of growth. The life of entrepreneurship has its' ups and downs, there are ebbs and flows of any business. But I chose (and still choose) to GROW through it, not simply go through it. I had to overcome a lot of self-doubt, adversity and I had to learn to let go of the "need of approval" from others. As a rising unstoppable woman entrepreneur, you will need to face fears, look adversity dead on, and make a decision about what is most important to you! Developing the daily habits needed for success is going to be a crucial turning point for you and your future!

These five habits will surely aid in your journey to becoming an unstoppable woman entrepreneur.

1. **Creating your vision**- focus on your vision for your future and THINK about it daily. When you think about it you must attach the emotion to the perceived outcome. You can create a Vision Board or Vision Book or type out a forecast "story" of the future YOU. These are helpful ways to stay dedicated to creating conscious thinking.

2. **Reading/Studying your craft**- whatever it is you are passionate about or working on in your business, read and study it! Listen to podcasts, watch videos, become a sponge soaking up the knowledge. Make sure to include personal and self-development reading and studying into this as well. Your income/success will only grow at the extent YOU grow.

3. **Journal**- journaling is a great way to tap into your creativity and it also can be therapeutic! It doesn't need to be perfect writing simply take time to write down what you are thinking about. You may be surprised at the creativity that comes out! Journaling is also a great way to write down daily gratitude (and practicing daily gratitude is life-changing too). This habit is also a great way to reflect on your journey, celebrate wins and learn from the past.

4. **Surround yourself with positivity:** Your circle of influence is crucial to your mindset, energy, and belief. Surround yourself with high vibe people and supportive women. Attend events and social gatherings that will fuel your fire and be uplifting to your soul. Sit at the table where women are talking about their dreams and goals, not gossiping about others. Be selective with whom you give your energy.

5. **Prayer**- if you do not have faith in God, this one may not resonate with you. Prayer has been the habit I credit most of my success with. Prayer is our access to our Creator. He created you and knows your desires and dreams. "You have not for you ask not." ASK the Lord and trust his guidance. Give the glory to God and he will continue to multiply it. Focus on the WHAT not the HOW. When we know WHAT we are working for and we partner with the Lord, the HOW always seems to show up. Typically, the HOW shows up in creative thought and serendipitous opportunities!

Remember queens, the sky is not the limit, your belief system is! Create a belief in self so strong that you inspire other women to do the same!

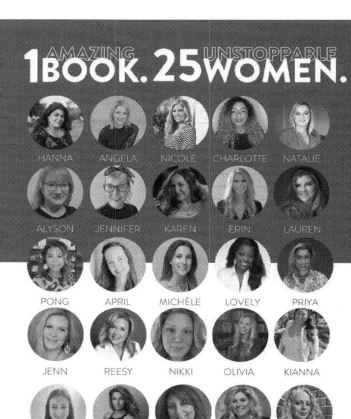

MADE BY MOMPRENEURS FOR MOMPRENEURS

Becoming An Unstoppable Woman Mompreneur is written for mamas who are already in business as well as for mamas who are ready to launch themselves into the entrepreneurial world. We believe that mompreneurs are leaders in business due to their resilience, compassion, and unwavering commitment to succeed. The amazing mama authors in this book have shared their truths, hearts, secret trade secrets, and so much more on none other than Mother's Day. The #BAUW authors celebrate all around the world in the hopes of sharing inspiration and celebrating our achievements as moms.

She Rises, She Leads, She Lives
Join the #BAUW Becoming An
Unstoppable Woman Movement.
www.SheRisesStudios.com

JOIN THE MOVEMENT!

#BAUW

Becoming An Unstoppable Woman

With She Rises Studios

She Rises Studios was founded by Hanna Olivas and Adriana Luna Carlos, the mother-daughter duo, in mid-2020 as they saw a need to help empower women around the world. They are the podcast hosts of the *She Rises Studios Podcast, the* TV show hosts of *Becoming An Unstoppable Woman*, as well as Amazon best-selling authors and motivational speakers who travel the world. Hanna and Adriana are the movement creators of #BAUW - Becoming An Unstoppable Woman: The movement has been created to universally impact women of all ages, at whatever stage of life, to overcome insecurities, adversities, and develop an unstoppable mindset. She Rises Studios educates, celebrates, and empowers women globally.

Looking to Join Us in our Next Anthology?

Becoming An Unstoppable Woman In Finance

Visit www.SheRisesStudios.com to see how YOU can join the #BAUW movement and help your community to achieve the UNSTOPPABLE mindset.

Have you checked out the *She Rises Studios Podcast?*

Find us on all MAJOR platforms: Spotify, IHeart Radio, Apple Podcasts, Google Podcasts, etc.

Looking to become a sponsor or build a partnership?

Email us at info@sherisesstudios.com

Made in the USA
Middletown, DE
24 May 2022

66134038R00110